FOOTBALL SUPERSTARS

Jerry Rice

FOOTBALL SUPERSTARS

Tiki Barber

Tom Brady

John Elway

Brett Favre

Peyton Manning

Dan Marino

Donovan McNabb

Joe Montana

Walter Payton

Jerry Rice

Ben Roethlisberger

Barry Sanders

FOOTBALL ⬤ SUPERSTARS

Jerry Rice

Jon Sterngass

CHELSEA HOUSE
PUBLISHERS
An imprint of Infobase Publishing

JERRY RICE

Chelsea House
An imprint of Infobase Publishing
132 West 31st Street
New York NY 10001

Library of Congress Cataloging-in-Publication Data
Sterngass, Jon.
  Jerry Rice / Jon Sterngass.
      p. cm. — (Football superstars)
  Includes bibliographical references and index.
  ISBN 978-0-7910-9607-9 (hardcover)
  1. Rice, Jerry—Juvenile literature. 2. Football players—United States—Biography—
Juvenile literature. I. Title. II. Series.

  GV939.R53S837 2008
  796.332092--dc22
  [B]   2008012410

Chelsea House books are available at special discounts when purchased in bulk quantities
for businesses, associations, institutions, or sales promotions. Please call our Special Sales
Department in New York at (212) 967-8800 or (800) 322-8755.

You can find Chelsea House on the World Wide Web at http://www.chelseahouse.com

Text design by Erik Lindstrom
Cover design by Ben Peterson
Composition by EJB Publishing Services
Cover printed by Bang Printing, Brainerd, MN
Book printed and bound by Bang Printing, Brainerd, MN
Date printed: March, 2010
Printed in the United States of America

10 9 8 7 6 5 4 3 2

CONTENTS

Simply the Best

In 1999, *The Sporting News*, a famous national sports magazine, attempted to pick "Football's 100 Greatest Players" of the twentieth century. The magazine even tried to rank the players based on their talent, their passion, and the excitement they brought to the football field.

Of course, any list ranking "great" football players will be open to debate. *The Sporting News* chose Cleveland Browns **running back** Jim Brown (1957–1965) as the greatest football player of all time. In the second position was Jerry Rice, a **wide receiver** who played most of his career with the San Francisco 49ers. The magazine chose Rice over every **quarterback**, yet the list was certainly not slanted toward wide receivers. Don Hutson of the Green Bay Packers (1935–1945) was listed No. 6, but then no other wide receiver appeared until the San Diego

Chargers' Lance Alworth (1962–1972) at No. 31. If Rice was not the greatest football player of all time, he certainly had almost no competition as the greatest receiver of all time.

Jerry Rice's career was so amazing that it is not unreasonable to argue that he was football's greatest player. Indeed, Mike Shanahan, his former San Francisco offensive coordinator and the Super Bowl-winning coach of the Denver Broncos, judged Rice as "the greatest player to ever play the game." There is plenty of evidence to support that position. When he retired, Rice held 38 NFL records, including career **receptions** (1,549), **yards** receiving (22,895), **touchdowns** (208), and touchdown receptions (197). He played in four Super Bowls, winning three championships and one Super Bowl MVP Award. Rice played in the **Pro Bowl** 13 times. Over his career, he played in 76 games in which he recorded at least 100 receiving yards.

For two decades, opposing defenses designed their game plans just to stop Rice. Yet he still owns the record for 274 consecutive games (more than 17 years!) with at least one reception. (Art Monk is second with only 183 consecutive games.) Almost all receivers would be thrilled to catch 77 passes in a year. Yet Rice averaged 77 receptions a year for *20* years.

One of Rice's most astonishing records is his 22,895 career receiving yards. Tim Brown, the great Oakland Raiders receiver, is in second place all-time. Yet Brown trails Rice by an unbelievable 8,000 receiving yards despite playing for 17 years himself. Most receivers would happily take the difference in yardage between Rice and Brown and call it a great career.

Rice dominated the wide receiver's position in the NFL for 20 years. There seemed to be nothing he could not do. He could catch short and long passes. He could turn short passes into long gains. One NFL coach, Dennis Green, called him "the best [pass] route runner I've ever seen." Rice was fearless over the middle and often outjumped **cornerbacks** for the ball. He was sure-handed in a crowd and an excellent blocker. New York

AN EXCELLENT ARGUMENT STARTER

Nothing generates controversy faster than ranking a group of people in any field. Here are the top 20 football players on *The Sporting News*'s list from 1999 of the 100 greatest professional football players of the twentieth century. Would Tom Brady make the list now? Peyton Manning? Randy Moss? Brett Favre? Start arguing.

1. Jim Brown (fullback, 1957–1965)
2. Jerry Rice (wide receiver, 1985–2004)
3. Joe Montana (quarterback, 1979–1994)
4. Lawrence Taylor (linebacker, 1981–1993)
5. Johnny Unitas (quarterback, 1956–1973)
6. Don Hutson (wide receiver, 1935–1945)
7. Otto Graham (quarterback, 1946–1955)
8. Walter Payton (running back, 1975–1987)
9. Dick Butkus (middle linebacker, 1965–1973)
10. Bob Lilly (defensive tackle, 1961–1974)
11. Sammy Baugh (quarterback, 1937–1952)
12. Barry Sanders (running back, 1989–1998)
13. Deacon Jones (defensive end, 1961–1974)
14. Joe Greene (defensive tackle, 1969–1981)
15. Gino Marchetti (defensive end, 1952–1966)
16. John Elway (quarterback, 1983–1998)
17. Anthony Muñoz (offensive tackle, 1980–1992)
18. Ray Nitschke (middle linebacker, 1958–1972)
19. Dick "Night Train" Lane (cornerback, 1952–1965)
20. John Hannah (offensive guard, 1973–1985)

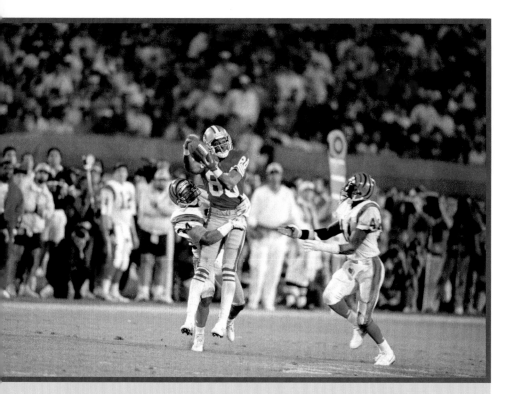

Jerry Rice pulls in a long pass during the fourth quarter of Super Bowl XXIII despite being covered by Cincinnati Bengals cornerback Lewis Billups *(left)* and safety Ray Horton. Rice caught a record 11 passes for 215 yards during the game on January 22, 1989, and he was named MVP of the Super Bowl.

Jets wide receiver Wayne Chrebet said in *The New York Times*, "He was the best and everybody knew it."

QUICK ON THE FIELD

Rice had only average speed for a wide receiver, according to the stopwatch. In this case, however, the clock lied. Rice, 6-foot-2 and 200 pounds (188 centimeters and 91 kilograms), may not have been a sprinter, but he had brilliant game speed. He could change direction, explosively and at full speed, better than almost any other receiver could. His extra gear often rocked even the swiftest cornerbacks back on their heels. Rice's breakaway speed made him a deep threat, but he regularly turned short **slants** into long gains and touchdowns.

Part of Rice's greatness was natural, but it was joined to a legendary attitude and work ethic. Rice blended talent with an addiction to training that made him the most feared receiver in the NFL. "We're all measured by how we do against Rice," said Robert Massey, a Pro Bowl cornerback. "I remember the first time an NFL scout talked to me right before the **draft**. The only thing he asked me was if I thought I could cover Jerry Rice."

Rice's need to prove himself was so great that he never let up and never felt satisfied. "It's all about competition, and I *love* competition," he said in his 2007 autobiography, *Go Long*. He admitted to constantly living in fear of not being able to measure up to his teammates' standards or his own. That fear drove him to practice and perform at levels far beyond other players. San Francisco quarterback Steve Young got to the Hall of Fame throwing to Rice. In describing Rice, Young said:

> When you were a kid . . . there was always one kid on your team who tried harder than the others. He might not have been the most talented kid, but he would huff and puff, and run extra laps, and do anything he could to help the team win. And the coach would always say, "If I had a hundred kids like that kid, we'd be world champions." Well, Jerry Rice is that kid, only taken to an insane degree. It's just that he has so much raw talent, people don't think of him that way.

Bill Walsh, who coached Rice with the 49ers, used the same image and extended it even further. "There are others that have the same dogged determination and perseverance but aren't able to do things because physically, they can't," Walsh said. "But I don't even think there's been a guy equal to him physically—even a so-called non-achiever, somebody where people would say, 'God, he'd have been great, if only he'd had a better attitude . . .' There isn't even one of those."

Randy Cross was an All-Pro **offensive lineman** who played with Rice on one Super Bowl winner with the 49ers. Cross said admiringly of Rice, "He is not a normal human being." Most people would agree. He was simply the best wide receiver ever to play the game of football.

That's What
Made Me

Jerry Rice was born on October 13, 1962, and grew up in Crawford, Mississippi. He was the sixth of eight children—six boys and two girls—born to Joe B. and Eddie B. Rice. For some famous people, it does not matter where they grew up. For Jerry Rice, it mattered a great deal.

Crawford is a very small town in Lowndes County in the east-central part of Mississippi. It is 100 miles (161 kilometers) from Birmingham, Alabama, and 115 miles (185 kilometers) from Jackson, Mississippi. The nearest big town, Columbus, is 20 miles (32 kilometers) away, and even Columbus only had about 20,000 people.

Rice later remembered that Crawford had "no stoplights, very few street signs, a few broken-down sidewalks, and not that many people—somewhere between five hundred and a thousand back when I was growing up." More than 90 percent of the townspeople were African American. In the center of Crawford, a 40-foot-long (12.2-meter-long) house trailer served as the town's city hall, library, and fire department. Before Rice, Crawford's most famous native son was Big Joe Williams (1903–1982), an African-American blues musician known for his unique style of playing his nine-string guitar.

"Growing up in a small town taught me the meaning of doing the right things," Rice later said in his 1996 book *Rice*. "Because the town was so small, if you did something wrong it was going to get back to your parents. And with my parents, that meant you would be disciplined, so I think it made me into a better person."

In colonial times, the area of eastern Mississippi where the Rice family lived was Chickasaw and Choctaw country. White settlers took over Native American lands in Mississippi after a series of treaties between 1805 and 1834. The rich land tempted Southern whites to try to raise cotton with slave labor. As early as 1837, African-American slaves made up 57 percent of Lowndes County's population. In 1860, the U.S. census recorded 16,730 slaves in the county, most engaged in cotton growing.

When slavery ended in 1865, many African Americans stayed on and tried to eke out a living on the land. In 1900, three out of every four Lowndes County residents were black. As the United States became more industrial and more urban, eastern Mississippi remained a backwater. In the 1970s, the Rice children were still handpicking cotton to earn some extra money to help the family.

A RURAL CHILDHOOD

There were some benefits to growing up in a rural area. The Rice family lived on seven acres in a house that Joe B. Rice had built with his own hands. The house was surrounded by waist-high brush and swampland. Paved roads were rare. There was no public transportation, and very few people owned cars. Jerry Rice walked or ran five miles (eight kilometers) to school every morning and five miles back every afternoon.

Jerry and his brothers also ran to try to catch the horses that roamed the open pastures of the local farms. The horses ran wild, so if someone wanted to ride a horse, he or she had to chase it down first. Catching a horse taught Rice the importance of patience. On a good day, it still took him almost an hour to chase down a horse. When he later became a star, Rice said of the town of Crawford, "That's what made me . . . running those back dirt roads and country fields."

Rice remembered his childhood as a mixture of positive and negative experiences. Rice's mother provided a caring environment even though Jerry did not own the newest toys and gadgets. In *Rice*, he remembered, "There was a lot of bad stuff going around—kids stealing cars, doing drugs—but I feel that my parents raised me the right way. . . . I think my upbringing molded me into the person I am today."

Rice's drive to excel came in part from his relationship with his father, a tough, proud, and stubborn man. Rice's father had a gentle side, but he could also be very mean and occasionally whipped Jerry. As a child, Jerry lived in fear of his father's judgments and anger. He later recollected, "As my dad aged, he grew harder and more angry. . . . He never came out and told me he was proud of me." For most of his career, Rice strove to win the respect that he never received from his father. He particularly was on the lookout for a "father substitute" who would provide acceptance without the fear he felt at home.

In *Go Long*, written after his playing career ended, Rice confessed that it was fear that drove him. He wrote:

It took me years to admit that fear is at the root of my performance. . . . My fear of failing as a child carried over onto the football field in high school and then college. I was so concerned about not being successful that it pushed me to be successful. All of those extra hours in the gym or on the track or on the practice fields were more than just about hard work; they were about avoiding failure. Before every game of my NFL career I was scared—scared to drop the big pass, scared I'd let my teammates down. And now I realize it all goes back to not wanting to disappoint my father.

As a football player in the NFL, Rice was famous for his excellent "hands." He rarely dropped passes that were thrown to him. Jerry developed some of his eye-hand coordination while working for his father, a skilled mason and bricklayer. During the hot summer months, the Rice boys helped Joe B. Rice build homes in the area. The brothers would work as the supply chain for their father, who actually laid the brick. It was the kids' job to make sure that the bricks were ready to be set and the mortar prepared. One of his brothers would stack about four bricks on top of each other and toss them up to the scaffold where Jerry worked. The thrown bricks might end up going in any direction. It was Jerry's job to catch them all. Jerry performed the job thousands of times for hours on end until he learned to grab all four bricks no matter where they went.

In the end, the grueling work improved Jerry's athletic skills. Pushing a wheelbarrow in the broiling Mississippi summer heat helped build his strength and stamina. More important, he learned the value of doing a difficult job to the best of his ability. He recalled, "My father was very demanding, and it was a challenge to keep everything running smoothly. We had to lay a certain number of bricks every day, so he'd really push everybody hard, no matter how sweaty we got. For me, it was a matter of pride."

But Jerry did not want to follow his father into the building trades. Like many teenagers working at their first physically demanding job, Jerry quickly realized that the work was not

During Super Bowl XXIII, Jerry Rice makes a finger-tip catch—his eye always on the ball. During his NFL career, Rice became known for his famous "hands." His extraordinary hand-eye coordination developed in part through helping his father lay bricks as he was growing up.

only difficult but also rather boring. Rice looked back on his short bricklaying career with pride, but he also said, "I remember thinking how this was not something I wanted to be doing for the rest of my life."

FINDING FOOTBALL

Jerry Rice did not originally see football as his destiny or even his route out of eastern Mississippi. He loved to play sandlot football and enjoyed watching the Dallas Cowboys on television. He especially liked wide receivers like Drew Pearson of the Cowboys and John Stallworth and Lynn Swann of the Pittsburgh Steelers. Rice loved "the way Swann would fly through the air and make those incredible catches. He wasn't a real fast guy but he ran great routes." Jerry, though, excelled at many sports. He did not even play football as a freshman at B.L. Moor High School in Crawford. His mother thought the game was too rough for Jerry, and that was that.

According to legend, Rice's football career began by accident. He was cutting a class one day in the tenth grade when the school's assistant principal spotted him in the halls. When Jerry heard his name called, he panicked and sprinted away. His speed and acceleration astonished the assistant principal. The next morning, the school's principal called Jerry into his office and offered to lessen the punishment if Jerry would report to the school's football coach. The coach, Charles Davis, talked Jerry into trying out for the team.

Jerry's mother was not happy. Eddie Rice still worried that Jerry would get hurt playing high school football. However, she recalled, "the more I fought it, the more determined he was, so I gave it up." Jerry's football career had begun.

As a football player at B.L. Moor, Jerry played several positions, including running back, **defensive back**, and even quarterback. His favorite position, though, was wide receiver. By the time he was a senior in high school, Jerry was an All-State selection at wide receiver in Mississippi.

Willie Gillespie regularly played quarterback for B.L. Moor High School. Jerry and Willie spent hours practicing together to perfect their timing on pass patterns. They even worked out on their own time after school practice had ended. Soon, Jerry and Willie developed a special feeling for what the other was going to do. This type of extraordinary chemistry between quarterback and receiver later became a trademark of Rice's career in college and in the NFL.

Jerry continued to play other sports in high school. His speed and coordination made him an excellent all-around athlete. He joined the track team as a high jumper and played forward on the basketball team. His best sport, though, was football, and not surprisingly, it became his clear favorite. The smallness of the community gave him a chance to shine.

A CHANGING WORLD

Jerry benefited from life in Crawford for another important reason. In this out-of-the-way African-American town, he was mostly isolated from the racism that dominated Mississippi society. He remembered, "I did have a few white friends, a few white classmates, but for the most part, blacks surrounded me."

The Mississippi that Jerry Rice was born into in 1962 was changing rapidly. Mississippi had been one of the most racist states in the nation. For example, the all-white basketball team from Mississippi State had been forced to turn down NCAA tournament bids in 1959, 1961, and 1962 because the state had a policy forbidding sports teams from its schools to compete with teams that had black players. In 1963, Governor Ross Barnett again banned the all-white Mississippi State basketball team from traveling to the NCAA tournament to play against Loyola (of Chicago) because Loyola's team had black players. This time, though, the Mississippi State players were angry because they wanted to play. Like in a spy movie, Mississippi State had to send a decoy team to divert the state police while the real team snuck out of the state on a private plane in the middle of the night. (After all that, Loyola beat Mississippi 61-51 and went on to win the NCAA basketball title in a shocking upset over Cincinnati). This all occurred the year after Jerry Rice was born.

The system of racial segregation that dominated Mississippi society had begun to crumble in the 1960s. In the "Freedom Summer" of 1964, hundreds of young volunteers from the North joined brave black Southern activists to establish "freedom schools" in Mississippi. They pushed African Americans to resist segregation. Civil rights workers such as Fannie Lou Hamer gave speeches and walked the back roads of the state encouraging black Mississippians to register to vote.

Unfortunately, many whites in Mississippi were unwilling to accept African Americans as their equals. In 1963, Mississippi civil rights leader Medgar Evers was murdered in his own driveway. The next year, white vigilantes bombed and burned several black churches in Mississippi. The violence climaxed with the murder of three civil-rights workers—James Chaney, Andrew Goodman, and Michael Schwerner—in Philadelphia, Mississippi. They were killed by a group of Ku Klux Klan members that included sheriff's deputies.

The sacrifices of the brave civil-rights activists in Mississippi were not in vain. They helped lead to the passage of the Civil Rights Act of 1964 and the Voting Rights Act of 1965. These laws had an immediate effect on Mississippi. Within a decade, the state's politics changed completely as white politicians now had to appeal to black voters if they wanted to get elected. In 1960, only 5 percent of African Americans in Mississippi were registered to vote. Only eight years later, 59 percent were registered to vote. Mississippi was changing.

The great breakthroughs of the civil-rights movement in Mississippi opened up opportunities for Jerry Rice. However, growing up in Crawford, most of the violence seemed far away. Of his childhood, Rice said in *Go Long*, "Sure, there

JAMES MEREDITH GOES TO COLLEGE

In 1962, James Meredith's simple attempt to enroll in college led to a revolution in higher education in the South. Meredith was born in Kosciusko, Mississippi, of Choctaw and African-American heritage. He served in the U.S. Air Force from 1951 to 1960 and then attended Jackson State for two years. Twice in 1961, the University of Mississippi rejected Meredith's application for admission. A federal court ruled that Meredith had been denied admission because of his skin color and ordered him admitted.

No African American had ever attended Mississippi's most famous school, known as "Ole Miss." The governor of Mississippi, Ross Barnett, firmly believed in racial segregation. He once said, "The Negro is different because God made him different to punish him." Barnett personally tried to prevent Meredith from registering for classes at Ole Miss. Barnett announced, "I have made my position in this matter crystal clear. … No school in our state will be integrated while I am your governor."

On Meredith's first day at the University of Mississippi, a rioting mob confronted him. Even U.S. marshals could not keep the peace. In a single night, 160 marshals were wounded (28 by gunfire), and two bystanders were killed by stray bullets. The next morning, President John F. Kennedy ordered 5,000 U.S. Army soldiers to the campus to keep the peace. The actions of the federal government revealed that the old days were gone in Mississippi. Meredith graduated from Ole Miss in 1963 with a degree in history. His enrollment there is one of the most famous moments in the history of the civil-rights movement. All this took place the year Jerry Rice was born and less than 20 years before he attended college in Mississippi.

U.S. marshals and troops escorted James Meredith *(center)* as he tried to attend classes in October 1962 at the University of Mississippi. Meredith was the first African-American student to enroll at the university—a milestone in the civil-rights movement.

was racism in Mississippi. We're talking about the 1960s and 1970s, a time when the civil-rights movement was under way but slow to reach parts of America. Yet growing up, I never once experienced racism firsthand. No one called me the N word, no one painted racist slogans on our home or burned a cross on our lawn; we were lucky." The worst Jerry experienced was "dirty stares if I walked into certain parts of the county that were predominantly white." Under these favorable conditions, Jerry reached the age when it was time to start thinking about college.

FEW COLLEGES INTERESTED

B.L. Moor High School was a small school. At the time, it had about 500 students spread out over 12 grades. The football team played on a field that seated only 100 people. B.L. Moor got very little publicity in the newspapers and television reports in Mississippi even though the team had a winning record.

Jerry Rice had a spectacular senior year in high school. He caught 80 passes and scored 35 touchdowns. This was especially astounding because high school football teams usually emphasize running the football. Moor High School went 18–2 in Rice's last two seasons. Rice remembered that "it was football that drove me and moved me, a game that was my great escape. As my athleticism improved . . . it began to occur to me that football could be my way out of Mississippi and the only life I knew."

Yet college scholarship offers did not pour in. It seemed as if no college appreciated the young player from Crawford. Tom Rice, one of Jerry's older brothers, was playing college football on scholarship at Jackson State University. Tom, a 6-foot-2, 275-pound (188-centimeter, 125-kilogram) center, told his coach that his brother was a really good wide receiver. Jackson State's offense, however, was built around running the football. Jackson State's coach was not interested in a skinny receiver from a rural high school.

Jerry actually wanted to go to Mississippi State University, a large school in Starkville just 20 miles (32 kilometers) from Crawford. Mississippi State, though, was not interested. More than 40 National Collegiate Athletic Association (NCAA) Division I-A schools contacted Jerry, yet none offered him a scholarship.

However, all was not lost. Archie Cooley, the coach of Division I-AA Mississippi Valley State University (MVSU), had heard about Rice. MVSU, located in little Itta Bena, Mississippi, was not a football power. This meant that Coach Cooley always needed to be on the lookout for underappreciated high school prospects. Cooley had a large network of African-American high school coaches helping him spot potential football players to give them a chance at a college education. One of Cooley's sources tipped the coach off about Rice, and Cooley made the trip to Crawford. Cooley was impressed by Rice, but Rice was even more impressed with Cooley. "No one else came to see me in person," Rice remembered.

At Cooley's invitation, Rice went to visit MVSU. Like most high school seniors, he based his judgment of the college on rather superficial things. He liked the football team's colors (green, red, and white). He loved the college atmosphere, with a raucous band and good-looking cheerleaders. With few other available choices, Jerry accepted the scholarship offer from MVSU and arrived in Itta Bena in the fall of 1981. He remembered thinking, "The future was on my shoulders . . . to make things better for our family, to build the new house, to get out of Mississippi, to make a better life. I wasn't so sure how I was going to do that, I just knew it was my destiny. I wasn't going to be a bricklayer."

Years later, when Rice was a world-famous athlete, he wrote, "I still return to Mississippi every summer, and sometimes we [his family] make additional trips during the year. It's important to us to maintain our roots and connection to the state, and it is even more important that our kids know where and how we grew up. Despite not always having the fondest memories of home, Mississippi is still home to me and forever will be."

The Satellite Express

J erry Rice had lived an isolated existence in his hometown. When he left high school, he attended a college that did not differ a great deal from where he used to live. Mississippi Valley State University (MVSU) was a mainly African-American school located in tiny Itta Bena, the hometown of legendary blues singer B.B. King. This is the heart of the Mississippi Delta, where a third of Mississippi's black population lives. The university is about 100 miles (161 kilometers) north of Jackson and 75 miles (121 kilometers) from Rice's home in Crawford.

MVSU was one of the lesser-known historically black colleges and universities in the United States. These were schools of higher education established before 1964 to serve the African-American community. For a "historically black college," MVSU did not have much of a history. The Mississippi state legislature had created its forerunner, Mississippi Vocational College, in 1946 on the site of an old cotton plantation. In 1964, the name of the institution was changed to Mississippi Valley State College. By the 1980s, it was a university with about 2,500 students on a 450-acre campus.

MVSU played in the Southwestern Athletic Conference against other historically black schools like Alcorn State and Jackson State in Mississippi, Grambling State and Southern University in Louisiana, and Prairie View A&M University in Texas. These were schools rich in football tradition from the days when white Southern schools refused to accept African-American football players (or students).

However, the MVSU football team, nicknamed the Delta Devils, was not a major power. From 1966 to 1977, the team suffered through 12 straight losing seasons. No Delta Devil player had ever been picked higher than the ninth round of the NFL draft. MVSU's only player of note was David "Deacon" Jones. Although Jones was one of the greatest defensive linemen of all time, he only attended the school for one year in 1960 and he was not drafted until the fourteenth round.

MVSU's football stadium only held about 10,000 spectators. Dirt patches covered the mosquito-infested practice fields. "You'd try to practice, and there would be mosquitoes all over you," Rice remembered. "We would go and buy Off and spray it all over ourselves, but that would only work for a time."

MVSU, however, gave Rice the chance to demonstrate his abilities. Many college teams emphasize running the ball more than passing it. But not MVSU, and its innovative coach, Archie Cooley. Cooley, hired at MVSU in 1980, was nicknamed the "Gunslinger" because of how often he had his quarterbacks throw the ball. MVSU quarterbacks routinely threw 50 passes a game. It was the perfect system for a receiver to show his stuff. Although Cooley was also a small-town Mississippi boy, Rice remembered that the coach lived up to his nickname. "He wore flashy clothes and a big cowboy hat," Rice said in *Go Long*. "When he walked into a room, he wanted the room to notice."

Like many young students, Rice took some time to adjust to college. When two of his friends returned to Crawford before school started, Rice wondered if he should be going with them. He said, "I missed the security of being home, but I didn't get on the bus. MVSU was part of my journey to a better life, and I wouldn't lose sight of that." In Rice's freshman season, he caught Cooley's eye instantly. The coach remembered, "The first week of practice, I knew Jerry was a special athlete because his work ethic was so great. He was the first one on the practice field, and he'd stay after practice." In his first year in college, Rice caught 30 passes, including two touchdowns.

Rice was also extremely lucky because his receivers' coach was Gloster Richardson, a former NFL player. Richardson, a Jackson State graduate, had never been a star in the NFL, but he had managed a solid eight-year career in which he won two Super Bowl rings—one with the Kansas City Chiefs and one with the Dallas Cowboys. Rice could not have had a much better tutor, and Richardson also admired his student. "He doesn't need to use his body to catch the ball," Richardson said. "His hands are just a gift." Rice felt that Richardson "taught me everything I needed to know about catching a football: how to watch it coming out of the quarterback's hands, how to cradle the ball against your body, and how to make that quick first step after the catch. I soaked up everything I could."

A TANDEM IN SYNC

As a sophomore in 1982, Rice had a new quarterback, a freshman from Leflore County, Mississippi, named Willie Totten. Totten's nickname was "Satellite" because the ball seemed to be constantly in orbit when he was playing. Totten and Rice together acquired the nickname "The Satellite

Express." The two of them became friends off the field and practiced football late into the evening. In *Go Long*, Rice remembered, "We worked on our routes, our timing, the height of the ball, our snap count, and just about every other aspect of the quarterback-wide receiver tandem."

Under Cooley, MVSU ran an unusual offense that featured four wide receivers. Sometimes they would all line up on one side of the field to mix up the defense. Other times, the receivers would line up behind each other in sets of twos. Cooley's offense was so unique that it usually baffled opposing defenses. As a result, Rice finished his second year by almost doubling his production to 66 passes for 1,133 yards and seven touchdowns.

In 1983, Rice's junior season, the Delta Devils posted a 7–2–1 record. This was the school's most wins since the 1965 season. The Rice-Totten combination, aided by big fullback Carl Byrum and little wide receiver Joe Thomas, carried MVSU into the national spotlight. Rice set numerous records that year, including NCAA marks for receptions (102) and receiving yards (1,450). He was named first-team Division I-AA All-America. He also set a single-game NCAA record by catching an astonishing 24 passes against Southern University.

NO HUDDLE, NO WORRIES

Amazingly, Rice's statistics had not yet peaked. In the summer of 1984, just before Rice's senior season, one of Archie Cooley's assistants had a brilliant question. He wondered aloud why MVSU's offense even bothered to huddle given that Totten often changed the play at the **line of scrimmage**. "Good question," Cooley replied. He suggested to Totten that he might as well start calling all his plays at the line of scrimmage without a huddle.

Many people who saw MVSU's "no huddle offense" thought it was insane. The lack of a huddle made it harder for the offensive players to know the plays. However, it also put pressure

Jerry Rice, shown in the stands of the stadium at Mississippi Valley State in November 1983, began to make a name for himself that season. He set NCAA records in 1983 for receptions and receiving yards. The following season, Rice would shatter those marks.

on the defense to make quick adjustments in strategy and prevented the opposition from making substitutions.

The Delta Devils quickly became the most entertaining team in the United States. The "run and shoot" offense set records in 1984 that still stood in 2008: most points per game (60.9), most yards gained per game (640.1), and most first downs per game (31.7). Looking back, Totten said, "It's amazing that some of those records are still standing. And we weren't even trying to set records. They just happened. We were just having fun." In one game, the Delta Devils trailed Southern University 36-6 at halftime and came back to win 63-45.

That season, MVSU won nine games, breaking the school record from the previous year. The Delta Devils defeated archrival Jackson State for the first time since the 1954 season (they would not beat the school again until 1994), as well as Southern and Grambling. This would be the only time that MVSU ever defeated those three schools in the same season. They also played before their largest crowd ever; 63,808 fans attended the showdown between MVSU and Alcorn State in Jackson's Veterans Memorial Stadium (won by Alcorn State, 42-28).

"To run our offense, you've got to have a quarterback who can throw it," Cooley said. The coach certainly had one in Totten. "The Satellite" would end his college career with a record-setting 139 career touchdown passes (47 of them to Jerry Rice). Totten was particularly brilliant in the no-huddle offense. Against Prairie View, he threw for a staggering 599 yards. Five times in Totten's career, he passed for more than 530 yards in a single game. Against Kentucky State in 1984, Totten threw *nine* touchdown passes (MVSU won 86-0). That season, Totten set the all-time single-season touchdown passes mark (56) for all divisions.

Rice was the chief beneficiary of this pass-happy attack. As a senior in 1984, he set 18 Division I-AA records. He broke his own records for receptions (112) and receiving yards (1,845). His 27 touchdown receptions set the NCAA mark for all divisions. In single games, Rice caught 17 passes for 199 yards against Southern and 15 passes for 285 yards against Jackson State. Against Kentucky State, he caught 12 passes and scored three touchdowns in one quarter. Rice finished his career with 301 catches for 4,693 yards and 50 touchdowns (some sources have the numbers as 310, 4,856, and 51). Rice's NCAA record for total career touchdown receptions stood until 2006 when it was broken by University of New Hampshire receiver David Ball.

Years later, Rice reminisced about the no-huddle offense. "I don't know where he [Archie Cooley] got it, but it brought so much attention to Mississippi Valley State," Rice said. "It was definitely ahead of its time. Then I noticed when I got into the pros they started running the same kind of offense with four receivers. They're still doing that today—trying to spread the field and take advantage of the defense."

Willie Totten was Jerry Rice's quarterback for three years at Mississippi Valley State, and together, they formed "The Satellite Express." During his college career, Totten threw a record-setting 139 touchdown passes (47 of them to Rice). Later, Totten, seen here in a 2003 photo, returned to Mississippi Valley State to be its football coach.

Even though Totten ran the madcap offense, Rice was the best player on the team. He acquired the nickname "World" because there did not seem to be a ball in the world he could not catch. He was named to every All-American team. He even finished ninth in **Heisman Trophy** balloting for the best college player of 1984. This was amazing for a player from such a small school without a football tradition.

THE PROS ARE WATCHING

Rice began to think he had a future in professional football. Some analysts believed that Rice was a definite first-round pick based on his astounding records at MVSU. Rice's performance

THE CIVIL WAR AS A FOOTBALL GAME

At one time, the Blue-Gray Game was one of college football's most famous bowl games. From 1939 to 2001, the game took place at the Crampton Bowl in Montgomery, Alabama. The game pitted players who attended college in the former Confederate states (the "Grays") against those who attended school in the rest of the country (the "Blues"). Throughout the civil-rights struggles of the 1950s and 1960s, the Blue-Gray Game continued to re-enact a sort of Civil War.

What made the Blue-Gray Game special was not its format but its timing. Before 1980, there were only five or six bowl games and those were mostly played on New Year's Eve and New Year's Day. However, the Blue-Gray Game was played on Christmas Day and was usually the first college all-star game each year. For this reason, most big-name college stars could not play in it because they were practicing for bowl games with their regular teams. As a result, players in the Blue-Gray Game came from teams with losing records or from smaller schools that did not play major college football. After the Blue-Gray Game desegregated in the 1960s, it also featured in the annual Blue-Gray Game, an all-star game for college seniors, also helped him. Rice's team won 33-6, and he played so well that he was named the game's MVP. NFL scouts admired Rice's outstanding performances on the field as well as his attitude.

On the other hand, Rice's detractors claimed that his college records had been set against inferior defenses and that he was a low pick at best. There were also questions about his speed, which tested at 4.6 for the 40-yard dash. Most scouts

many African-American stars (like Jerry Rice) from historically black colleges.

In an era before cable television and 24-hour sports replays, the Blue-Gray Game gave lesser-known players an opportunity to be noticed by NFL scouts who may not have had the chance to see them play in person. A short list of some of the stars who have played in the game includes Bart Starr (Alabama), Len Dawson (Purdue), Fran Tarkenton (Georgia), Bruce Smith (Virginia Tech), Norm Snead (Wake Forest), Napoleon McCallum (Navy), Don Maynard (Texas Western), Howie Long (Villanova), and Curtis Martin (Pittsburgh).

Unfortunately, the vast increase in the number of college bowl games helped doom the Blue-Gray Game. Very few college stars are even relatively unknown in a *SportsCenter* world and there are fewer surprises in the NFL Draft each year. The last real Blue-Gray Game took place in 2001. After a year off, the game was revived in 2003 in Troy, Alabama. It was soon discontinued again and now lives on only in the memories of football fans.

wanted a wide receiver to run 4.3 or 4.4. They thought that Rice was not fast enough to play in the NFL. They claimed that anyone with a little talent could rack up big statistics while playing for a small school. No one from MVSU had ever really succeeded in the NFL. According to *Go Long*, Rice had his own doubts: "During my senior season, I'd often play head games with myself, at times convincing myself that I could be great at the pro level while at other times pointing to all the great players who never made it, including my brother."

Rice did have a backup plan if football did not work out. "I was good with my hands," Rice said in his 1996 memoir, "so I wanted to go into something like electronics. I could always fix things—if something was broken, I could look at it and mess around with it and get it to work. I'd fix toasters, radios, television sets, anything that plugged in." As a kid, Rice thought about opening his own fix-it shop one day. At MVSU, Rice majored in electronics and earned a B average. Still, he hoped he would not have to use his college degree in the immediate future.

DRAFT UNCERTAINTY

When draft day finally arrived in the spring of 1985, Rice was still not sure where he might be picked. Rice recalled, "I can remember the anticipation of the draft, being so nervous and not knowing what's going to happen." NFL drafts could be hard to predict. In 1983, NFL teams chose six quarterbacks in the first round. Yet in the next two years, no quarterbacks were chosen at all in the first round. In 1985, Rice watched as eight of the first nine picks were either offensive or defensive linemen. Then two wide receivers were taken—Al Toon at No. 10 and Eddie Brown at No. 13. Both went on to have excellent NFL careers, although neither reached Rice's level.

While Rice tried to figure out what would happen next, he received a call from the San Francisco 49ers telling him that the team was about to draft him as choice No. 16. Rice was

Coach Bill Walsh *(right)* and the San Francisco 49ers celebrated in the locker room in January 1985 after their victory in Super Bowl XIX. Walsh began to keep track of Jerry Rice after seeing him play on television in the fall of 1984. Some football insiders thought that Rice was too slow to play pro football, but Walsh believed otherwise.

shocked. The 49ers were the defending Super Bowl champions, a team with stars like Joe Montana, Ronnie Lott, Roger Craig, and Dwight Clark. Only recently, Rice had watched these players on television. In *Go Long*, he remembered that "they epitomized for me what football was all about: the love of the game, the professional approach, and the desire to win. I had just wanted to go *somewhere* but this was the perfect situation."

He wasn't the only one who was thrilled. Bill Walsh, the 49ers head coach, was equally excited to be able to draft Rice. Walsh was considered an excellent judge of talent. According to legend, Walsh first saw Rice on television in October 1984 while watching football highlights in a Houston hotel room. He was so impressed, he began to follow the wide receiver from MVSU. The 49ers coach believed that Rice was more than just a small-school, gadget-offense product and that Rice's supposed lack of speed would not be a problem.

Because the 49ers had won the Super Bowl, they had the last pick in the first round of the draft. It seemed unlikely that Rice would be left at No. 28. When Rice was still available midway through the 1985 draft, Walsh decided to trade up to get him. He offered the New England Patriots his first-, second-, and third-round draft picks in exchange for the Patriots' first-round No. 16 pick and third-round selection. The Patriots accepted, and the 49ers drafted Rice with the sixteenth pick in the 1985 NFL Draft.

Rice was excited to be drafted, but he still had doubts about his own abilities. He remembered thinking, "Could I compete at the NFL level, particularly with the reigning Super Bowl champions? How could I survive in such a big city when all I had known were the fields of Mississippi? Would I fail in the NFL and have to face my old friends and family and become a bricklayer in Mississippi?"

Meanwhile, the "Gunslinger" era lasted one more year at MVSU. As a senior in 1985, Totten led MVSU to a 7–2 record and ended his college career holding more than 50 records. Other than Rice, none of his MVSU teammates had successful professional playing careers. Archie Cooley only lasted as coach of MVSU through the 1986 season; he would never recapture the success of his years with the Delta Devils.

MVSU had been the perfect springboard for Rice to achieve his dream of a professional football career. In the spring of 1999, the "Satellite Express" was recalled when MVSU changed the name of its football stadium to Rice-Totten Field. Totten was inducted into the College Football Hall of Fame in 2005, followed the next year by Rice. Totten returned to MVSU to become head football coach in 2002, and Rice visited him on campus during the football season after Rice's retirement.

"It was so weird because it was just like yesterday," Rice said in *USA Today*. "The second I stepped on campus, I knew right where to go and where to hang out. I try to keep up with Willie and help out with shoes and uniforms—anything I can do to give back to Valley."

From "Butterfingers" to Rookie Sensation

The San Francisco 49ers that Jerry Rice was joining were one of the greatest teams in NFL history. In 1984, San Francisco's defense had allowed the fewest points (227) in the league. For the first time in NFL history, all four members of the 49er **secondary** (the players who defend against passes)—Ronnie Lott, Eric Wright, Dwight Hicks, and Carlton Williamson—had been selected to play in the Pro Bowl.

In the playoffs, the 49ers defeated the New York Giants 21-10 and then shut out the Chicago Bears 23-0 in the NFC Championship Game. For a grand finale, the 49ers cruised to victory in Super Bowl XIX against the Miami Dolphins, 38-16. In the game, the 49er defense dominated record-setting quarterback Dan Marino while San Francisco quarterback Joe Montana won his second Super Bowl MVP Award. The

38

49ers finished the game setting a bunch of Super Bowl records, including most yards gained (537). It was the 49ers' second championship in four years. They had finished the year with a record of 18–1.

San Francisco had not always been a football power. Although they had joined the NFL in 1950, the 49ers had never won an NFL championship until the 1980s. In fact, they had not even won a division title until 1970. The team's turnaround began in 1979 with the hiring of Bill Walsh, formerly the coach of Stanford University, to be the 49ers head coach. Walsh turned out to be an inspired choice. Among other abilities, Walsh had a reputation for making excellent draft selections.

Jerry Rice was arguably Walsh's best-ever draft pick. "I thought Jerry would be picked in the first five selections in the draft," Walsh said in *Rice*. "But as we talked to our colleagues in the NFL, somehow, some way, he had run a 4.6 40 [40-yard dash in 4.6 seconds]. So he had been downgraded. It was easy for scouts to dismiss Jerry because of his time. Because otherwise, they would have had to project a player from Mississippi Valley State as a major NFL contributor, and that's a tough one to sell to management and coaches. This way, they could deflect the idea by saying, 'Well, it's a small college, and he has a slow time.'"

TRAINING-CAMP CHALLENGE

When Rice came to training camp in 1985, he was challenging wide receiver Freddie Solomon for a spot in the starting lineup. Solomon was a respected veteran, 10 years older than Rice, and coming to the end of a fine career. However, Solomon remained an outstanding receiver. In 1984, he caught 40 passes for 737 yards (18.4 yards/catch) including 10 touchdown catches. Solomon had 12 more receptions in the postseason with two more touchdowns.

Walsh had hoped that Rice would replace Solomon as soon as possible. Yet Solomon was not bitter. He even helped Rice at several key points in his **rookie** year. The surprised Rice said that Solomon "really showed a lot of character. It is very hard when you know you are at the end and someone has come in to take your job. But he and Dwight [Clark] passed the torch on."

Clark, the other receiver ahead of Rice, was 28 years old, an All-Pro, and in the prime of his career. Clark noticed the new rookie immediately. He observed that Rice "was raw but he just had the ability to get his hands on the ball, no matter where he was and no matter who was covering him."

Clark was already an NFL legend. In the 1981 NFC Championship Game, the 49ers trailed the Dallas Cowboys 27-21 with five minutes remaining. The 49ers were on their own 11-yard line when Montana led San Francisco on a long drive all the way to the Cowboys' 6-yard line. On a third-and-three play, Montana threw the ball off balance to Clark in the **end zone**. Clark seemed to soar in the air high above any defenders and caught the ball for a touchdown and the 28-27 victory. Most football fans simply know the play as "The Catch." The 49ers then defeated the Cincinnati Bengals in Super Bowl XVI to complete one of the most amazing turnarounds of any franchise in NFL history. Under Bill Walsh, the team had gone from back-to-back 2–14 seasons to a Super Bowl championship in just two years.

Jerry Rice first met quarterback Joe Montana in training camp. By this time, Montana was a two-time Super Bowl MVP. Rice remembered, "I had watched him on television. I had seen him make so many incredible plays and pull out so many last-minute victories. I was a little bit in awe." For the next six seasons, Montana and Rice would form one of the greatest quarterback-receiver combinations in NFL history. "I thought a guy of his status would be conceited, not give me the time of day," Rice thought. "But it was the opposite. He was very relaxed and willing to talk to you and help you out in any way possible."

Joe Montana and Jerry Rice formed one of the greatest quarterback-wide receiver combinations in football history—a bond that began to develop in training camp in 1985. "I was a little bit in awe," Rice said about first meeting Montana, who had already won two Super Bowls. Here, Montana *(right)* blocks for Rice during a playoff game in January 1989 against the Minnesota Vikings.

Nonetheless, Rice was a little frazzled by his new lifestyle. The country boy from Mississippi was now plunked down in one of America's most sophisticated cities. When he flew to San Francisco after being drafted, it was the first time he had ever been on an airplane and he was scared stiff. Coming from a small town and a small college, he now had to face the expectations of being a first-round draft choice on a Super Bowl winner. Rice thought, "I'm coming to this big city, and there's nobody that I know. I wanted to turn around and go back on the plane, go back home." Over it all hung the question as to whether a kid who compiled big statistics at Mississippi Valley State could make it in the NFL.

For his agent, Rice had chosen Eric Glenn, whose clients included Willie Gault, possibly the fastest wide receiver of all time. "All along," Rice said, "I wanted to sign with a black agent. I wanted to give a black agent the opportunity to do something big." Rice and Glenn negotiated a five-year contract with San Francisco worth $1.8 million. The big rookie contract gave Rice access to a celebrity lifestyle with which he was unfamiliar.

When Rice reported to the 49ers training camp at Sierra College in Rocklin, California, he surprised a few people by arriving with an expensive car with license plates that spelled W-O-R-L-D, his college nickname. Rice claimed he was simply trying to project confidence. "All I've really got to do," he said, "is just catch the football and read defenses." Running back Roger Craig remembered that in Rice's first year, "Jerry didn't come in and boast that he was the best receiver in the league. He just kept his mouth shut and kept working hard."

"WEST COAST FATHER"

Rice was helped by the fact that Bill Walsh liked and believed in him. Walsh was always more than just a coach to Rice. "For me, Bill was like a father," Rice said in *Go Long*. "I could talk to him about football, about relationships, about the business of being a professional athlete. He even had the same body language of disapproval that my own father had: that stern look, that crossing of the arms, that raised eyebrow. . . . I never wanted to let my father down, and now I never wanted to let Bill down." Rice began to refer to Walsh as his "West Coast father," a man he could respect without fearing.

Rice excelled for San Francisco in the preseason. He was now wearing No. 80, instead of the No. 88 he wore in college. The rest of his game, however, seemed the same. Facing Pro Bowl cornerback Lester Hayes in a preseason game, Rice caught three passes for 49 yards. Two weeks later, he caught five passes for 125 yards against the San Diego Chargers, including a 56-yard touchdown reception. After the game, Rice said,

"When I was drafted out of Mississippi Valley State, the word was I had good hands, could get open, and ran well when I got the ball. But they also said I wasn't really a speed-burner. Today, though, I think I showed I can get down the field in a hurry."

Jerry Rice caught his first NFL pass in San Francisco's first regular-season game of the 1985 season against the Vikings in Minnesota. "It's hard to explain the feeling of being surrounded by 60,000 screaming fans," he reminisced in *Go Long* about his first game. "The big games I played in college were certainly nothing like this. But amazingly, I wasn't nervous. I had been dreaming about this for a long time."

Rice began the season playing superbly. He averaged 22 yards per catch in his first three games, including three catches for 94 yards in a 34-10 win over the Oakland Raiders. Walsh rewarded Rice by moving him into the starting lineup ahead of Freddie Solomon. In the fifth week, Rice caught three passes, including a 25-yard touchdown, in a win over the Atlanta Falcons.

A ROOKIE LETDOWN

Then Rice began to slump. He dropped important passes in losses to the Bears and the Lions. He was often wide open when balls bounced off his hands. Rice dropped at least 10 passes in his first 10 games, many at the worst possible times. Soon, fans and the press began to question whether he was a wise draft pick after all. Teammates sometimes called him "Butterfingers." By the tenth week, Solomon had his starting job back and Rice was on the bench. Forty-Niner assistant coach Paul Hackett said, "We thought initially that we could find the right balance between the use of Freddie and Jerry. But after the Raiders game, where Jerry did so well, we just thought he really had arrived. Now, the pendulum has swung the other way."

Rice's confidence began to wane. Maybe he wasn't good enough to make it in the NFL? He remembered, "Oh, man, there were many games where I just went in and cried. I cried

Jerry Rice moved the ball downfield during a game on October 13, 1985, against the Chicago Bears. During the game, Rice dropped key passes—beginning a slump that would last much of the mid-season. Rice began to lose confidence and wondered if he belonged in the NFL.

because I had always been able to catch a football and make a play, and now I was dropping footballs and I just couldn't pinpoint what was going on." A *San Francisco Chronicle* article from October 1985 compared Rice unfavorably to the other rookie wide receivers. Rice had 18 catches for 295 yards at that point while Eddie Brown of the Cincinnati Bengals had 29 catches for 469 yards.

On November 17, the 49ers played the Kansas City Chiefs in San Francisco and Rice played perhaps the worst game of his career. In the first half, Montana threw him two passes. Both times, Rice was wide open. Both times the ball hit his hands and fell to the ground. The hometown fans booed loudly. In the locker room, Rice began to sob. Several teammates, and even Bill Walsh, had to come over and calm him down. Walsh remembered, "He came in at halftime, and he was far more affected by it than I expected. . . . He had broken down and was very emotional and very hurt."

Nonetheless, the 49ers were beating the Chiefs 31-3. With five minutes remaining in the game, the coaching staff decided that Rice needed a confidence boost. Since he had yet to catch a pass in the game, they called for an easy short pass to him. Rice caught it, ran eight yards downfield, and then **fumbled**. The boos rained down on Rice. Teammates again had to encourage him to keep his head up and keep working hard.

The season was not going well for the 49ers either. The Super Bowl champions were only 6–5 and in danger of missing the playoffs. Of course, Rice was not solely responsible for the team's problems. However, he was one of the easiest players to blame. If the defense was getting old and Montana's passing numbers were off, those players had at least helped San Francisco to a Super Bowl victory in the previous season. On the other hand, Rice was a rookie who had cost the team several draft picks, had replaced a well-liked and productive veteran, and was now dropping half the balls thrown to him. The worst thing for Rice was that he agreed with most of the criticism. In *Rice*, he said, "Joe [Montana] is a very patient guy, but when he's putting the ball right there on the money he feels like you should catch the football, and I kept dropping it."

In a press conference after the Kansas City game, Walsh defended his use of Jerry Rice over Freddie Solomon. He told an unhappy San Francisco area media that the 49ers' troubled rookie wide receiver would remain a starter despite his problems holding onto the football. "At some point, the boos will turn to cheers," Walsh predicted.

But why was Rice dropping so many passes when he had never had this problem before? Everyone seemed to have a different theory. Some people claimed that Rice was thinking about scoring touchdowns before securing the ball. Others claimed that Rice was not being worked enough in practice. Bill Walsh thought that Rice might have been "hearing footsteps."

At first, Rice believed his dropsies might have been caused by the gloves he began to use when he joined the 49ers. But Rice later rethought the problem. In *Go Long*, he said that "when I started dropping balls . . . I took [the gloves] off, thinking the gloves were the issue. But I dropped passes even without gloves. It was then that I realized that it wasn't the gloves but my lack of focus that was at the root of the problem."

Just days after Walsh defended him, Rice had another horrible game. In front of 57,000 home fans, Rice dropped three more passes. The 49ers defeated the Seattle Seahawks 19-6, thanks in part to a 27-yard touchdown catch by Solomon. Walsh tried to find Rice new ways to get the ball. Against the Washington Redskins the next week, Rice took a **reverse hand-off** and ran 77 yards for a touchdown. Unfortunately, a **holding penalty** wiped out the play. Although the 49ers won 35-8, Rice went through the entire game without a pass reception for the second time in his brief career. Those few weeks were the lowest point of Rice's career.

MONDAY NIGHT CURE

It all turned around in the fourteenth week. On December 9, San Francisco was playing a Monday night game against the Los Angeles Rams to decide the NFC West Division title. A national television audience saw Rice catch 10 passes for 241 yards, a team record at the time. In the third quarter, Montana saw Rice covered only by safety Nolan Cromwell. Cromwell was a Pro Bowl player, but Rice still caught a 66-yard touchdown to give the 49ers the lead. Later in the game, Montana again saw Rice in single coverage and threw a 52-yard completion that led to a touchdown. The 49ers lost the game, 27-20, but Rice felt relieved. "When it was over," he recalled, "I knew I could play professional football." Fellow receiver Dwight Clark noted, "He made the All-Rookie team in one night. The frustrations of the first 13 games all disappeared and everything clicked."

A leaping Jerry Rice snagged a pass during the 1985 season finale against the Dallas Cowboys. In the last few games of the season, Rice rebounded from his slump. Against the Cowboys, he caught seven passes for 111 yards and scored a touchdown on a reverse.

The Rams defenders were also impressed. "I think the nick-name that man's got, 'All-World' or whatever, is deserved," said Los Angeles safety Johnny Johnson after the game. "The man's got unbelievable speed and a great burst." Local writers who thought Rice was a bust suddenly changed their minds.

The following week, Rice gained 82 receiving yards against the New Orleans Saints. In the season's last game, he caught seven passes for 111 yards against the Dallas Cowboys. He even scored a touchdown on a reverse, which helped the 49ers clinch a spot in the NFL playoffs. By Christmas, Rice had become a possible candidate for Rookie of the Year. (Eddie Brown of the Bengals, one of the two wide receivers taken ahead of Rice, won the award.).

RATING THE ROOKIES

Throughout his rookie season, Jerry Rice faced comparisons—not always favorable—to other first-year wide receivers. Two receivers, Al Toon and Eddie Brown, were picked ahead of him in the draft. Here's a look at the statistics the three compiled during their rookie seasons.

	TEAM	G	R	Y	Y/R	TD
Jerry Rice	SF	16	49	927	18.9	3
Eddie Brown	CIN	16	53	942	17.8	8
Al Toon	NYJ	15	46	662	14.4	3

And here's a look at the career statistics for the three players.

	R	Y	Y/R	TD
Jerry Rice (20 seasons)	1,549	22,895	14.8	197
Eddie Brown (8 seasons)	363	6,134	16.9	41
Al Toon (8 seasons)	517	6,605	12.8	31

In the first round of the playoffs, the 49ers faced the New York Giants. San Francisco gained 362 yards of total offense, with Clark catching eight passes for 120 yards. Rice contributed four receptions for 45 yards. Yet the Giants limited San Francisco to only one **field goal** and defeated the 49ers, 17-3.

So Rice's rookie season ended with this playoff defeat. Yet he had much to be proud of. Despite his problems catching the ball, he had finished with 49 receptions for 927 yards. He had made an impact in the NFL. He was a starter on a playoff team. The future looked bright.

Mastering His Trade (1986–1987)

Bill Walsh's reputation as a brilliant head coach stemmed from his pick of quarterback Joe Montana in Walsh's first draft in charge of the 49ers. Montana had led Notre Dame to the 1977 NCAA national football championship and to a number of dramatic comeback victories. Most scouts, however, did not think Montana was a top prospect. He was relatively slow and small for a quarterback without great arm strength. Montana was still available in the third round of the draft when Walsh selected him (the eighty-second player taken). It turned out to be a steal. Montana's success in the playoffs, and his ability to lead the 49ers to big comebacks, made him perhaps the best quarterback ever to play the game.

After drafting Montana, Walsh provided him with an offensive system that maximized his ability—the so-called **West**

Jerry Rice left behind two Minnesota Viking defenders after catching a pass during a game in 1986. Bill Walsh's offense relied on short passes, and Rice often turned those receptions into big gains, creating a new offensive category—yards after the catch.

Coast offense. This offense was more an approach to the game than a set of plays or formations. Walsh's team specialized in short, quick passes, usually no more than a few yards. Receivers ran precise routes, often to a specific spot. Plays were usually timed to the fraction of a second. A quarterback like Montana (and later Steve Young) was perfect for this type of offense. He could make quick decisions and throw highly accurate passes to exact locations off a very quick drop.

Using short passes, Montana and Young would lead the league year after year in completion percentage. Some seasons, the 49ers quarterbacks would complete more than two-thirds of their passes. Walsh's short passing system brought out the best in Jerry Rice, as well as other San Francisco players, such as receivers Dwight Clark and John Taylor, **tight end** Brent Jones, and running back Roger Craig. Rice turned those short passes into a new NFL category: "yards after the catch." The statistic became necessary because of all the times Rice would catch a short slant and sprint downfield for a long gain or touchdown. "The old-line NFL people called it a nickel-and-dime offense,"

BILL WALSH'S MISNAMED "WEST COAST OFFENSE"

Bill Walsh actually devised the so-called West Coast offense while working in the Midwest as offensive coordinator of the Cincinnati Bengals (1968–1975). However, Walsh's San Francisco 49ers won Super Bowls in 1981, 1984, and 1988 using his ideas. As a result of San Francisco's success, the scheme picked up the name West Coast offense even though Walsh always objected to the name. The phrase is now so widely used in football that it has lost all specific meaning. Over the years, coaches have adjusted, changed, simplified, and added to Walsh's offense.

Traditional offenses of the 1970s tried to establish their running game first. This would draw the defense up to the line of scrimmage and open passing lanes downfield. At that time, the passing game was based on a quarterback dropping back deep from the line of scrimmage and waiting for receivers to become open.

Walsh's offense, however, reversed the ideas of the traditional offense. San Francisco used passes to set up the running game, not vice versa. Walsh's system emphasized horizontal passes to help stretch the defense across the field. With the

Walsh said. "They, in a sense, had disregard and contempt for it, but whenever they played us, they had to deal with it."

The West Coast offense needed a quarterback who could get rid of the ball quickly. Montana, when forced to make a decision, more often than not looked for Rice. Montana noted, "Even if the coverage was tight, you knew he would be working hard and you knew that, if you stuck it in there, you'd have a pretty good chance of completing it. In tight situations, when

defense concentrating on short passes, Walsh's offense then made longer throws or ran the ball.

Walsh's offense also used the short, three-step quarterback drop instead of more traditional seven-step drops or **shotgun** formations. Most San Francisco pass plays occurred within 15 yards of the line of scrimmage. The plays unfolded very quickly, and the three-step drop helped the quarterback get the ball out faster and resulted in far fewer sacks. Short passes meant Walsh liked agile running backs who could catch the ball as well as run with it. San Francisco running back Roger Craig was the first back to gain 1,000 yards rushing and 1,000 yards receiving in the same season.

Several of Walsh's assistant coaches with the 49ers moved on to other teams and spread the use of his system. Mike Holmgren won a Super Bowl with the Green Bay Packers and coached in another with the Seattle Seahawks. Holmgren's assistant, Jon Gruden, coached the Tampa Bay Buccaneers to a Super Bowl victory. George Seifert later won two Super Bowls with the 49ers. One of Seifert's assistants, Mike Shanahan, won two Super Bowls with the Denver Broncos. All used some version of the misnamed West Coast offense.

the game was close, there were times I'd throw balls to him that I might not throw to anyone else."

As Rice began to learn the complexities of the offense and the pass routes, he became almost impossible to defend in single coverage. In 1986, Rice caught 86 passes and led the NFL with 1,570 yards and 15 touchdowns. It was the first of six seasons that Rice would lead the league in receiving yards and touchdown receptions.

However, the New York Giants crushed the 49ers in the 1986 playoffs, 49-3. The game resulted in one of Rice's most embarrassing moments. On the 49ers' first drive of the game, Rice caught a pass from Montana and appeared to be on his way to a 50-yard touchdown. Unbelievably, Rice fumbled the ball without anyone near him. The ball rolled all the way to the end zone for a touchback. The Giants took over and drove 80 yards to score. Later in the first half, Montana suffered a concussion and the 49ers fell apart.

Rice was extremely disappointed with his performance. "I can still see that ball just rolling along the ground," he remembered in *Rice*, "That play really changed the momentum of the game." Rice tried to turn the experience into a positive lesson. He learned that in a situation like that, a receiver had to "secure the football and don't relax until you get across that goal line." Rice was slowly mastering his trade. In the next 18 years, he had only 24 fumbles.

A BABY AND MARRIAGE

Rice began his third year in the NFL by marrying his girlfriend, Jackie Mitchell, on September 8, 1987. The two had first met on the MVSU campus in 1984 when Rice was a college senior and Mitchell was a high school senior. The couple had a daughter, Jaqui Bonet, in June 1987 and both felt the time was right to get married. Married life gave Jerry Rice a sense of stability, but he was not the easiest person to live with. Rice himself admitted, "The biggest adjustment for

Out in the clear, after making a sure touchdown catch, Jerry Rice fumbled the ball in the first quarter of a 1986 playoff game against the New York Giants. Soon after, quarterback Joe Montana was injured, and the 49ers unraveled, losing 49-3. From that game on, though, over 18 more seasons, Rice had only 24 fumbles.

Jackie was coming to terms with my internal drive for perfection. I didn't know any way else to succeed. . . . In our first 10 years of marriage, we never traveled . . . we never took advantage of what we could have done, because all I did was eat and sleep football."

At least Rice's determination paid off. The 1987 season was one of the best years in Rice's career. In that season, he set the NFL record for most touchdown receptions in a regular season with 22. Rice had at least one scoring reception in all 12 of his regular-season games. In the eleventh game, he caught two touchdown passes and broke the record of 18 set by Mark Clayton of the Miami Dolphins in 1984. He even ran for a touchdown in that game, a 35-7 win over Atlanta. Rice caught only 65 passes in 1987; more than one-third of his receptions went for touchdowns.

Rice's record lasted 20 years until December 29, 2007, when Randy Moss of the New England Patriots broke it with his twenty-third touchdown reception. Yet some people argue that Rice's record should still be recognized. That is because Rice set his record in just 12 games in 1987 when a players' strike shortened the season. Moss needed a full 16 games to break Rice's record. The loss of his record even annoyed Rice: "The only thing that bothers me a little bit is that I did it during the strike year," Rice said in *USA Today*. "It was 12 games for me. If he [Randy Moss] had done it in 12 games, I wouldn't have a problem with it at all."

THE PLAYERS WALK OUT

The 1987 season had been interrupted when the established NFL players went on strike and the owners replaced them for three games with scabs. (A scab is a person who refuses to honor a strike and crosses a picket line to work where the strike is taking place.) So Jerry Rice, Steve Young, and other members of the team found themselves walking on a picket line while so-called replacement players pretended they were the San Francisco 49ers. Many fans called them the "Phony-Niners."

The players' strike resulted from football's rapid growth in the 1970s. Television networks were setting all-time ratings highs showing NFL games. Advertising revenues multiplied two and three times. With the influx of money, football franchises became worth fortunes. Old-time family ownership began to disappear, replaced by new millionaires and billionaires who saw the NFL as a business and a sports team as a high-profile investment.

Like many business owners, the NFL's team owners hated competition. They knew a bidding war for players would simply raise salaries and reduce profits. Since 1961, the NFL teams had practiced revenue sharing. This meant that all teams split the network television money equally. Revenue sharing allowed NFL teams to exist in cities as different as New York and Green Bay because national broadcast rights provided all teams with an equal economic base. (The national television deals are still by far the greatest source of income for NFL teams; each team received almost $100 million in 2007.) Revenue sharing, however, meant there was little economic incentive for one team to try to outbid another team for players. Since all teams received the same share of the money, there was little economic difference between winning and losing.

For this reason, the NFL players thought that they were being exploited. The average playing career in the NFL was (and is) incredibly short—less than four years. While some exceptional players like Jerry Rice have long careers, most players leave the game because of injury or being cut by a team. In addition, while the NFL publicized multimillion-dollar contracts like Rice's, it did not highlight the fact that many lesser players earned much less. The average player's salary in 1981 was about $60,000 a year (in 2005, in contrast, it was $1.4 million).

If the NFL was making billions in the 1980s, the players felt they deserved a bigger share of the pie. In 1982, the NFL season was reduced from a 16-game schedule to nine games as a result of a 57-day players' strike. During this time, no NFL games took place at all. The strike was finally settled by a compromise agreement that ran through the 1986 season. This deal gave the players a percentage of the NFL's revenues and established minimum salaries for players based on their years of experience. Despite this success, many NFL players still wanted true free agency. Free agency meant that the players could sell their services to the highest bidder.

For a brief moment in the 1980s, football players had a choice where they could play. From 1983 to 1985, the United

States Football League (USFL) was formed to compete with the NFL. The USFL signed top-notch talent like Heisman Trophy winners Mike Rozier and Herschel Walker, as well as Steve Young, Doug Flutie, Reggie White, and Jim Kelly. Rivalry between the USFL and the NFL meant that football salaries began to rise—from an NFL average of $90,000 in 1982 (after the strike) to $230,000 in 1987. The USFL folded in 1985, however, and the NFL again faced no real competition.

When the NFL's labor contract ran out in 1987, the NFL Players Association asked the owners for true free agency as well as 55 percent of the gross revenues (in 2007, they received about 65 percent). Since the USFL had gone out of business, the owners again had a monopoly and saw no reason to negotiate. The players decided to go on strike after the second week of the season.

Jerry Rice supported the strike; that's why Rice's record of 22 touchdown catches in a season was broken by Moss, who played in an extra four games. Of the strike, Rice remembered, "We immediately began to picket outside our practice facility and Candlestick Park on game days. . . . We had to make it difficult for the replacement players, whom most of us disliked. How could anyone take someone's job during a strike? I didn't feel bad for the scabs . . . they had invaded our sacred area."

The players did not realize that the situation in 1987 differed from 1982. In that strike, the networks paid the owners in advance for the television rights. In 1987, the owners would not receive television money unless the games took place. So although NFL games scheduled for the third weekend were canceled, the games in Weeks 4, 5, and 6 were played with replacement players. The television networks displayed these games as if the hastily assembled teams were actually the same quality as a regular NFL team. A few veterans also crossed the picket lines, including Lawrence Taylor, Tony Dorsett, Howie Long, and Danny White. Many 49ers were annoyed when stars like Joe Montana, Roger Craig, and Dwight Clark broke players' ranks to play with the scabs.

Faced with cracks in its members' support and the willingness of the networks to broadcast the bogus games, the union voted to go back to work after 24 days. The same day, however, the players filed an antitrust lawsuit against the NFL (which the players eventually won) claiming that the league was an illegal monopoly.

Montana was one of the most famous scabs. (In contrast, Steve Young supported the strike.) In the 1982 strike, Montana refused to back the NFL Players Association. In fact, he did not even join the union, claiming, "Hell, why should I support something I don't believe in?" In 1987, Montana declared in advance of the strike that he was willing to cross picket lines. Randy Cross, a star offensive lineman for the 49ers, was San Francisco's player representative for the union. As he famously noted, "The NFL, like life, is full of idiots."

STILL A GREAT YEAR

Despite the missing games, Rice won NFL Player of the Year honors in 1987. His personal highlight-film moment occurred when the 49ers played the Bengals in Cincinnati in the second game of the year. The 49ers trailed in the fourth quarter with six seconds to play. The Bengals had the ball, fourth-and-two, on the 49ers' 25-yard line. All the Bengals had to do was punt and run out the clock. Yet for some reason, they tried a running play. They did not get the first down and the San Francisco offense got the ball back with two seconds left in the game. Montana told Rice he was just going to throw the ball up there and Rice would have to go and catch it. Somehow, Rice jumped as high as he could and came down with the ball. The 49ers won 27-26 and the play instantly became known as the "Hail Jerry" pass.

In the last six games of the 1987 season, Rice caught an incredible 14 touchdown passes. His heroics helped lead the 49ers to a 13–2 record. San Francisco was ranked No. 1 on both offense and defense; in the last three games of the season, the

Jerry and Jackie Rice posed for a picture after Jerry was presented with the Schick Trophy as the NFL Player of the Year for 1987. He set an NFL record with 22 touchdown receptions, despite playing only 12 games in a strike-shortened season. The Rices also were married in 1987.

team outscored its opponents a total 124-7 touchdowns. Most people felt the 49ers would win the Super Bowl.

Instead, the 49ers suffered one of the greatest football upsets of all time when they lost in their first-round playoff game to the 8–7 Minnesota Vikings. Minnesota's 36-24 victory marked the third straight year that the 49ers did not score a touchdown in a playoff game with Montana on the field. The 49ers eventually replaced Montana with Young, who scored one rushing touchdown and threw for another. But it was too little, too late. Despite their great season, San Francisco would not be going to the Super Bowl in 1987.

The 49ers were stunned. "We were the hottest team after the strike; then came that Minnesota game," remembered offensive guard Guy McIntyre. "I remember coming into the locker room and everybody just staring at each other. It was over that quickly." Randy Cross felt that loss was indirectly "part of the strike." As it turned out, the Washington Redskins went on to win Super Bowl XXII that year. It was more than a coincidence that, unlike the 49ers, none of the regular Redskins players crossed the picket lines during the period of scab games.

By the end of Rice's third year, he was a genuine NFL superstar. He was now 6-foot-2, 200 pounds, but he moved with the speed, acceleration, and agility of a much smaller man. He felt extremely comfortable with Montana as quarterback. In *Go Long*, Rice said, "Joe and I had such great chemistry on the field; we just knew what each other was thinking and what we needed to do to make the other's job easier." In 1987, Rice had led the NFL in scoring, the first receiver to do so since Elroy "Crazy Legs" Hirsch in 1951. He extended a streak of consecutive games with at least one touchdown to an NFL record 13. Yet he had played three years for the San Francisco 49ers and still not made it to a Super Bowl. For Rice, this was the one missing piece of the puzzle.

Super Bowl Hero
(1988–1992)

San Francisco had made the playoffs in the three seasons between Super Bowl XIX and Super Bowl XXIII, but the team was eliminated each time in the first round. Some people blamed poor performances by the 49ers' offensive stars. In those games, Joe Montana, Jerry Rice, and Roger Craig all failed to produce a single touchdown. Rice, in particular, had been less than stellar. In those three games, he had totaled a mere 10 catches for 121 yards and no touchdowns. Some fans questioned whether he was a "big game" player. Rice heard the gossip and was determined to excel. He knew that the greatest receivers, like Lynn Swann, Fred Biletnikoff, and John Stallworth, had made their reputations by performing in playoff games and the Super Bowl.

In 1988, Rice had one of the best seasons of his career. He caught 64 passes for 1,306 yards and nine touchdowns. His 20.4

yards-per-catch average would be the highest of his career. Yet the team struggled. At one point, the 49ers were 6–5 and in danger of missing the playoffs. However, they won four of their final five regular-season games. Craig had 2,036 combined rushing and receiving yards, earning him the NFL Offensive Player of the Year award.

PLAYOFF PROWESS

In the first round of the playoffs, San Francisco gained a little revenge for the previous year's upset by crushing Minnesota, 34-9. The team's offensive stars made a mockery of the claims that they could not produce in the playoffs. Montana threw three touchdowns to Rice (2, 4, and 11 yards) in the first half alone, and Craig rushed for 135 yards and two touchdowns as the 49ers routed the Vikings.

The 49ers then traveled to Chicago for the NFC Championship Game. The Bears played at Soldier Field, one of the few cold-weather stadiums without a dome. The temperature at game time was 17°F (-8°C) with a wind chill of -26°F (-32°C). In *Go Long*, Rice remembered, "After the first few offensive plays of the game, I realized I had a huge advantage over the defensive players trying to cover me. Because the field was mostly frozen outside areas along the sideline, I ran many routes along the boundary because it was hard for them to cut across the frozen field. I knew where I was headed, they didn't."

In the first quarter, the 49ers faced a crucial third down on their own 39-yard line. Despite the high winds, Montana completed a pass to Rice, who broke free of two defenders, and scored a 61-yard touchdown. Midway through the second quarter, Rice caught a slant and scored untouched for a 27-yard touchdown. Rice finished the game with five catches for 133 yards as the 49ers upset the Bears, 28-3. Despite the freezing conditions, the 49ers gained 406 total yards of offense.

The 49ers' win over the Bears gave San Francisco its third trip to the Super Bowl, to play the Cincinnati Bengals. The Bengals' offense, led by NFL MVP quarterback Boomer Esiason, had led the league in scoring, rushing yards, and total yards. One of their most potent threats was wide receiver Eddie Brown, who had been selected three picks ahead of Jerry Rice in the 1985 draft.

SUPER COOL

Rice was excited to be playing in the Super Bowl. In fact, he was too excited. Rice had always been a big believer in visualization.

THE YEAR THE SUPER BOWL DID NOT SELL OUT

The Super Bowl is the championship game of the National Football League. It is now the most-watched U.S. television broadcast of the year. About 100 million Americans tune in for at least some part of the Super Bowl. The game, identified by Roman numerals, has become a huge spectacle with a famous halftime show. Many people hold "Super Bowl parties," and the day is virtually a national holiday.

It was not always like this. The first Super Bowl, played on January 15, 1967, between the Green Bay Packers and Kansas City Chiefs, was not even a sellout. The game was part of an agreement between the NFL and its younger rival, the American Football League (AFL). The formation of the AFL in 1960 had led to a price war for players. As football players' salaries rose, the owners of the two leagues decided to merge. One condition of the AFL-NFL merger was that the winners of each league would meet to determine the "world champion of football." According to legend, the name "Super Bowl" was suggested by AFL founder and Kansas City Chiefs owner Lamar Hunt.

The night before a game, he would run his routes over and over in his head until he finally fell asleep. But now, as he wrote in *Go Long*, "in the hours before playing in my first Super Bowl, sleep was nowhere to be found. I was up in the middle of the night, pacing the carpet in my hotel room. My mind was filled with images of the game I was about to play in."

The Super Bowl is often an anticlimax, and many of the games have been one-sided romps. Super Bowl XXIII, however, was one of the best Super Bowls of all time. The score was tied 6-6 in the third quarter when the Bengals returned a kickoff

The first Super Bowl was far from the spectacle it is today. Only 62,000 people (in the 94,000-seat Los Angeles Coliseum) watched the Packers beat the Chiefs, 35-10. Amazingly, no known complete videotape of the game exists, even though two networks televised it. As of 2007, a two-minute clip is the only footage remaining of the first Super Bowl.

The NFL's Green Bay Packers won the first two Super Bowls fairly easily. Some team owners wanted to call off the merger since the AFL teams did not seem to be as good as the NFL teams.

That perception changed after Super Bowl III. In one of the biggest upsets in sports history, the AFL's New York Jets, behind Joe Namath as quarterback, defeated the Baltimore Colts. The next year, the AFL's Kansas City Chiefs defeated the NFL's Minnesota Vikings. This was the last game played between the champions of the two independent leagues, as the NFL and AFL officially merged in 1970.

93 yards for a touchdown to give Cincinnati a 13-6 lead. The 49ers responded with a touchdown of their own on a four-play, 85-yard drive. First, Montana threw a short pass to Rice, who turned it into a 31-yard gain. Then the San Francisco quarterback completed a 40-yard pass to Craig, moving the ball to the Bengals' 14-yard line. Montana's next pass was nearly intercepted, but he then threw a touchdown pass to Rice, who made a spectacular catch to tie the game.

The Bengals eventually took the lead, 16-13, by kicking a field goal with 3:20 remaining in the game. After a penalty on the kickoff, the 49ers took over on their own 8-yard line with only 190 seconds left in the game. The 49ers seemed to be in trouble.

Montana was unfazed. He led the 49ers on an 11-play, 92-yard drive to score the winning touchdown with seconds remaining. In the huddle just before the game-winning drive, Montana supposedly pointed to someone in the crowd and said, referring to a famous comedian, "Hey, isn't that John Candy?" The line became the most famous of Montana's career and sealed his reputation as the "coolest" quarterback in NFL history. Rice later said in *Go Long*, "I honestly can't confirm or deny that comment because I was so focused on moving the ball ninety-two yards with limited time that any extraneous comments would have been lost on me." However, Rice noted, "In that situation, there was no one you wanted at quarterback more than Joe Montana. He was typically calm, while calling out two plays in every huddle, while squatting down and picking grass."

Mixing passing and running plays, the 49ers cleverly moved the ball downfield. On the ninth play of the drive, the 49ers had second down and 20 on the Bengal 45-yard line with just 1:15 left in the game. Rice ran a square route across the middle, beat three defenders to the ball on the 33, somehow dodged them all after the catch, and ran to the 18-yard line. An eight-yard pass to Craig advanced San Francisco to the 10-yard line.

With 34 seconds left in the game, everyone thought Montana would try to pass to Rice. Rice had caught three passes for 51 yards in the drive and was the obvious target. Instead, Bill Walsh called a play in which Rice was the decoy and not the primary receiver. Montana hit John Taylor with a perfect 10-yard touchdown pass, giving the 49ers the win by a 20-16 final score.

In the 49ers' game-winning drive, Montana completed eight of nine passes for 97 yards (penalty yards included). For the game, he completed 23 of 36 passes for a Super Bowl-record 357 yards and two touchdowns. Craig finished the game with 71 yards rushing, and eight receptions for 101 receiving yards. He was the first running back in Super Bowl history to gain over 100 receiving yards.

Rice's performance in Super Bowl XXIII was even more remarkable. Rice celebrated his first Super Bowl by catching 11 passes for 215 yards and a touchdown. His receptions and receiving yards were both Super Bowl records. For his performance, he became only the third wide receiver (to that time) to earn the Super Bowl MVP.

Super Bowl XXIII was also the final NFL game coached by Bill Walsh. He finished his coaching career with the 49ers with a 102–63–1 record with three Super Bowl victories. His defensive coordinator and handpicked successor, George Seifert, took over head coaching duties. In *Go Long*, Rice said, "It hurt me tremendously to see Bill move on. I had laid it all on the line for him every day. I would have run through a brick wall for that man. He was the one who gave me the opportunity with the 49ers, and he was my West Coast father."

Normally, Rice's performance in the Super Bowl would have been the big story for days after the game. Only Montana had once again been clutch, John Taylor had made the big catch, and Bill Walsh had retired. As a result, even though Rice was the Super Bowl MVP, he had to share the postgame attention and publicity with others.

Sitting on the hood of his new car, Jerry Rice holds up the MVP trophy he won during Super Bowl XXIII against the Cincinnati Bengals. In the last minutes of the contest, during a 92-yard game-winning drive, Rice caught three passes for 51 yards. He was only the third wide receiver to be named Super Bowl MVP.

Rice felt that he was not getting his proper respect, not to mention endorsement opportunities. In a television interview, Rice bitterly claimed that "if it was Joe Montana or Dwight

Clark [winning the Super Bowl MVP], it would be in headlines all over." Twenty years later, Rice did not regret his remarks. He wrote in *Go Long*: "If a white superstar had been the Super Bowl MVP, things would have been different, with more attention from the media and the fans.... Simply being a black athlete, I have always felt I've had to prove myself and be very successful just to be accepted."

NEW COACH, SAME RESULTS

Seifert proved to be an able replacement for Walsh. The next season, he guided the 49ers to an NFL-best 14–2 regular-season record. The team's two losses were only by a combined margin of five points. San Francisco's offense had one of its best years in 1989. Montana threw for 3,521 yards, 26 touchdowns, and only eight **interceptions**. Rice also had a great year, catching 82 passes for 1,483 yards and 17 touchdowns. Running back Roger Craig was the team's leading rusher with 1,054 yards. Rice loved playing on this team. He said, "Joe, Roger, and I formed an impressive threesome. Before we ran onto the field prior to games, Roger would say, 'You take care of the air, and I'll take care of the ground.' And of course, Joe took control of it all."

Yet there was more to the 49er offense than the "Big Three." Wide receiver John Taylor had a fabulous season, catching 60 passes for 1,077 yards and 10 touchdowns. Tight end Brent Jones caught 40 passes for 500 yards. Fullback Tom Rathman had the best year of his career, rushing for 305 yards and catching 73 passes for 616 yards. Even Montana's backup, quarterback Steve Young, who saw time in 10 games, had a fantastic season, passing for 1,001 yards and eight touchdowns with only three interceptions. With all of these weapons, San Francisco's offense led the league in total yards (6,268) and scoring (442 points). At the same time, the 49ers defense ranked third in the NFL in fewest points allowed (253).

In the first round of the 1989 playoffs, the 49ers crushed the Vikings 41-13. On the 49ers' first play from the line of scrimmage, Montana completed a short pass to Rice, who sprinted all the way to the end zone for a 72-yard touchdown reception. By halftime, the 49ers led 27-3; Rice caught six passes for 114 yards and two scores. In the NFC Championship Game, San Francisco blew out the Los Angeles Rams by a 30-3 score. In the game, the 49ers had 442 total yards and held the ball for almost 40 minutes.

So for the second year in a row, Rice and the 49ers would be playing in the Super Bowl. This time, their opponents would be the Denver Broncos, led by quarterback John Elway. The 49ers were favored to win, but the final score of Super Bowl XXIV shocked even San Francisco fans. The 49ers annihilated the Broncos 55-10 and set a record (still standing in 2008) for points scored and widest margin of victory in a Super Bowl.

On their opening possession, Denver punted after only three plays. The 49ers scored on their first drive, marching 66 yards and scoring on a 20-yard touchdown pass from Montana to Rice. The Broncos responded with a field goal, but then the 49ers completely took over the game. A 38-yard touchdown pass from Montana to Rice increased the 49ers' lead to 27-3 at halftime. In the second half, the 49ers intercepted Elway's first pass of the third quarter, and Montana threw a 28-yard touchdown reception to Rice on the next play.

San Francisco's dominance was total. Rice caught seven passes for 148 yards and a Super Bowl-record three touchdown receptions. Montana set several Super Bowl records and won his third and last Super Bowl MVP award ("in a vote that could have gone either way," said Rice). San Francisco gained 461 yards of total offense and scored eight touchdowns in the game. At the same time, the 49er defense limited the Broncos to 167 yards, 12 first downs, and a time of possession of 20:29.

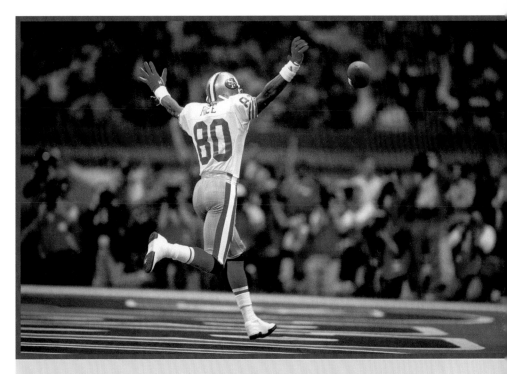

Jerry Rice celebrates as he scores a touchdown in Super Bowl XXIV—one of three touch-downs he had that day. In the game, on January 28, 1990, the 49ers demolished the Denver Broncos 55-10. The records for most points scored in a Super Bowl and biggest winning margin still stood in 2008.

The 49ers championship team of 1989–1990 was one of the best football teams of all time. The Niners won their three playoff games by a combined 100 points and finished the year 17–2. San Francisco is considered "The Team of the Eighties," winning four Super Bowls in the decade and missing the play-offs only twice. In Rice's two Super Bowls, the 49ers outgained Cincinnati and Denver by 914 yards to 396 yards.

ANOTHER TITLE?

Could the 49ers "three-peat"? In 1990, they won their first 10 games, and again finished an NFL best 14–2. Rice had another superb season, leading the NFL in receptions (100), receiving yards (1,502), and receiving touchdowns (13). It would be the only time in his career that he led the league in all three categories.

He played his best game against the Atlanta Falcons in October. The Falcons kept blitzing, and Montana kept hitting Rice in single coverage. By the time the shootout ended, the 49ers had won 45-35, and Rice had caught 13 passes for 225 yards and five touchdowns. Montana set team records with 476 passing yards and six touchdown passes. "It's tough duty for anyone to cover Jerry all day long, even when you have help," Montana said. "Anytime you see single coverage [on Rice], you know your chances are about 95 percent you're going to get a touchdown."

A third consecutive Super Bowl victory seemed entirely possible. In the first round of the playoffs, the 49ers beat the Washington Redskins 28-10. San Francisco, though, met its match in the NFC Championship Game against the New York Giants. The 49ers led 13-12 in the fourth quarter and simply had to run out the clock to make the Super Bowl. However, Roger Craig's fumble with 2:36 left in the game led to a game-winning field goal as time ran out.

Despite the success of the 49ers over the last three years, some of the team's stars were aging and becoming increasingly injury-prone. One hallmark of San Francisco's success had been the team's ruthlessness. When players got old, regardless of their past contributions, they were released to make way for new players. Now, after the 1990 season, the 49ers pushed Roger Craig and Ronnie Lott to leave the team. Rice was not happy. He said, "I understood that the NFL was a business, but I was still sad not to have those guys on my side."

Rice was now a six-year veteran in the prime of his career. With Craig and Lott gone, Rice took on more of a leadership role. He began to talk more in meetings and push his teammates harder. San Francisco cornerback Eric Davis noted the difference in Rice. Davis said, "There was a changing of the guard. He went from a quiet guy who never said anything and just did his job to a guy who felt like it was his time, who felt like he could speak out for what he believed in."

In addition to the turnover in players, the team suffered in 1991 when Montana missed the entire season with an elbow injury. But whether it was Montana, Steve Young, or Steve Bono throwing the passes, Rice was as steady as ever. He finished the season with 80 catches and 1,206 yards. The 49ers won their last six games but failed to make the playoffs despite a 10–6 record. This was the first time in Rice's seven-year career that he had missed the playoffs.

By 1992, an enormous quarterback controversy dominated San Francisco football. Montana was aging and increasingly injury-prone. Young was erratic and had an athletic style that did not always contrast positively with Montana's style. Third-string quarterback Steve Bono had played extremely well when called on. One of them had to go. But which one?

Rice wanted to catch passes from Montana. He came out publicly to support the four-time Super Bowl winner. "Joe had meant so much to the organization and had shown such loyalty that I only thought they should return the loyalty." Then it turned out that Montana would not recover in time to start the 1992 season. Young ended up as the starting quarterback and led San Francisco to a 14–2 record. Young finished the season with 3,465 passing yards and 537 rushing yards, along with an NFL-best 25 touchdown passes. Although he was technically still Montana's backup, he won the NFL's MVP Award.

For Rice, the 1992 season was notable for his breaking Seattle Seahawks receiver Steve Largent's career touchdown record. Rice caught touchdown No. 100 to tie the record against the Philadelphia Eagles on November 29. The next week, he caught the record-breaker from Young against the Miami Dolphins.

In the first round of the playoffs, San Francisco defeated the Washington Redskins 20-13. The 49ers then lost the NFL title game, 30-20, to the eventual Super Bowl champion Dallas

Jerry Rice trotted down the field after he scored his 100th touchdown catch on November 29, 1992, against the Philadelphia Eagles. With that catch, he tied Steve Largent as the NFL leader for most career touchdown receptions. A week later, Rice broke the record.

Cowboys. Even though San Francisco had 415 yards of total offense, the team committed four critical **turnovers**. Rice caught eight passes for 123 yards including a five-yard touchdown in the fourth quarter. The touchdown was his thirteenth in the playoffs, an NFL record. This did not make the loss any easier to take.

At the end of the 1992 season, San Francisco once again had to face the same quarterback controversy. Montana had helped the team win four Super Bowls in the 1980s. But there was no room for sentiment. The 49ers decided to keep Young and traded Montana to the Kansas City Chiefs before the 1993 season. "The trade happened so fast," said Rice, "none of us had time to react."

Rice was directly critical of the 49er organization for the Montana trade. He later said in *Go Long* that "I never got the chance to say good-bye, and Joe never had a chance to address his teammates. . . . He was the San Francisco 49ers and should have been treated better. . . . At the very least, the 49ers should have treated Joe with class." Rice, like everyone else, now had to accept that the 49ers had put the ball in Steve Young's hands.

Taking Nothing Away from Steve (1993–1999)

With Joe Montana at Kansas City, Jerry Rice would now have to catch passes from Steve Young on a permanent basis. Rice admitted that he was "quite skeptical, to be honest, when Steve stepped into the starting quarterback role." Young's early professional career had been a disaster. He signed a record contract with the United States Football League, but his team went bankrupt after two years. He then joined the Tampa Bay Buccaneers, who posted a 2–14 record in each of Young's two seasons with them. Fans, the press, and management all agreed that Young was a bust, and Tampa Bay traded him for two draft choices to the 49ers in 1987. It turned out to be a bad decision. Young spent the final 13 years of his career with the 49ers, leading them to a Super Bowl title and himself to the Hall of Fame.

Rice immediately noticed two things that made Young quite different from Montana. "First of all, he was left-handed," Rice observed in *Go Long*, "meaning everything would change for me, as I had never caught passes from a lefty in my life." To adjust to a left-handed quarterback, Rice spent hours on the practice field catching balls thrown by the 49ers' equipment manager, who happened to be a lefty. Rice never totally adjusted: "With a lefty, the ball comes out of the hand with a reverse spin that I wasn't used to—the ball spins to the left. When the ball met the palms of my hands, it just felt different."

Secondly, Young was a superb athlete with an ability to "scramble" away from the pass rush. This was a big change for San Francisco's wide receivers. Rice knew that, with Young as quarterback, "if I didn't get open quickly, he would tuck the ball under his arm and take off himself. Joe was more patient in the pocket, allowing us more time to get free."

Rice, however, eventually adapted to Young's style. He admitted that "Steve had a bullet arm and could drill the ball like John Elway or Brett Favre." And he couldn't argue with the results. In 1993, Young led the 49ers to a 10–6 record and set team records for most passing yards (4,023) and consecutive passes thrown without an interception (189), while leading the NFL in touchdown passes (29).

Rice also had a phenomenal year, catching 98 passes for 1,503 yards and 15 touchdowns. For his season, Rice earned NFL Offensive Player of the Year honors (for the second time). As of 2007, he was the only wide receiver ever to win the honor even once in the 35 years it has been awarded.

San Francisco advanced to the NFC Championship Game again by blowing out the New York Giants 44-3 in the divisional round. This set up another meeting with the Dallas Cowboys. There was considerable bad blood between the two teams. Rice did not like what he perceived as the Cowboys' arrogance. Before the game, he pleaded with his teammates

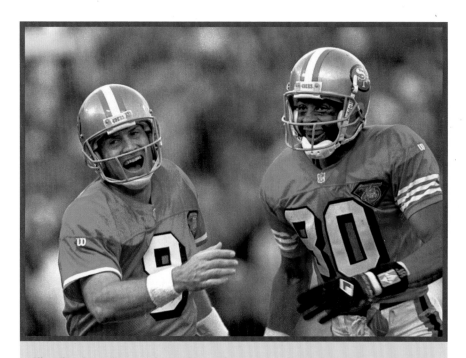

All smiles, Steve Young and Jerry Rice rush to congratulate tight end Brent Jones after Jones scored a touchdown against the Dallas Cowboys in November 1994. After years of playing with quarterback Joe Montana, Rice had to adjust to Young, who was left-handed and more of a scrambler than Montana.

that if they had any pride at all, they had to beat the hated Cowboys.

Rice had come a long way from his shy rookie days. Coach George Seifert observed, "Has he become more of a leader? Yes, absolutely. He has matured immensely. . . . He'll talk to the team before a big game. Or if we lose and he feels the team didn't put out the way it should, he's probably the first to reprimand the team." Young simply said, "There's a strength now to what he does. Instead of just the consummate player, he's now the consummate leader."

However, even Rice's passion was not enough as the 49ers lost to the Cowboys 38-21. Rice caught six passes for 83 yards but no touchdowns. At one point, he became so frustrated that he shoved a cornerback after a play and the referees penalized him for a **personal foul**. After the game, he bitterly admitted, "I certainly wasn't proud that we had lost two years in a row with a Super Bowl berth on the line."

SHORING UP THE DEFENSE

The 49ers organization knew that some changes had to be made. From 1988 to 1993, the 49ers played in five out of six NFC title games and won two Super Bowls. The team, though, had now lost two consecutive NFC Championship Games to the Dallas Cowboys. Management pinpointed the 49ers' shaky defense as the weak link. As a result, San Francisco brought in several veteran **free agents** from other teams to strengthen their defense before the 1994 season. Among the players signed were **defensive lineman** Richard Dent, **linebackers** Rickey Jackson and Ken Norton, Jr., and cornerback Deion Sanders.

In order to pay all their stars, the 49ers asked some players to renegotiate their contracts to free up salary-cap money. Some free agents, like Jackson and Sanders, accepted very low one-year salaries to play on a team with a chance to win the Super Bowl. Many critics complained that San Francisco was trying to "buy a championship" by playing with the NFL's free agent rules. The strategy worked, though. The free agents enabled the 49ers to jump from the 15th-ranked defense in the league to the 8th, and to rise from the league's 16th-best defense against the run to the 2nd.

Because of the new players, the 49ers could not afford to pay the five-man practice squad. Rice donated $170,000 to fund the practice squad. Rice said, "I felt like we needed those guys to get us ready. It was weird because the practice-squad guys all came up to thank me. I hadn't even thought of it that way."

Rice's first game of the season was historic. Against the Los Angeles Raiders, he finished with seven receptions for a season-high 169 yards and two touchdowns while running for one more. His last touchdown moved him into first place all-time in the NFL record books for career touchdowns with 127. This broke the record set by Cleveland Browns running back Jim Brown.

San Francisco, however, then had some problems. The 49ers lost 24-17 to the Kansas City Chiefs, led by former 49ers quarterback Joe Montana. After a 40-8 home loss to the Philadelphia Eagles, the majority of 49er fans wanted head coach George Seifert fired and Steve Young traded. Young would never have the respect of most 49er fans until he proved he could win a Super Bowl like Montana.

As it happened, the loss to the Eagles was the turning point of the season for the 49ers. The team rallied around Young to win 10 straight games, including a 21-14 victory over the arch-enemy Dallas Cowboys. During those 10 games, San Francisco's average margin of victory was nearly 20 points per game. The 49ers finished with a 13–3 record and Steve Young won the NFL MVP Award for the second time. He led the NFL for the third time in a row with 35 touchdown passes, while throwing only 10 interceptions. He also set a single-season 49er record for completion percentage (70.3 percent). Behind Young's great season, the 49ers led the NFL in total points scored (505). Rice was once again the team's leading receiver with a then career-high 112 catches for 1,499 yards and 13 touchdowns. John Taylor added 41 receptions for 531 yards and five touchdowns, and tight end Brent Jones caught 49 passes for 670 yards and nine touchdowns.

ANOTHER COWBOYS SHOWDOWN

In the NFL divisional playoffs, the 49ers easily defeated the Chicago Bears 44-15. The victory set up a third-straight 49ers-Cowboys NFC Championship Game. Most people also felt this game would be the "real" Super Bowl because those two teams seemed vastly superior to any AFC team. The 49ers absolutely hated the Cowboys; Dallas had knocked them out of the Super Bowl the last two years and then won it themselves.

This time, the result was different. The 49ers took a 21-0 lead less than eight minutes into the first quarter, benefiting from three Cowboy turnovers. The Cowboys fought back to 24-14 with two minutes left in the first half. However, with eight seconds remaining in the half, Young threw a perfect 28-yard touchdown completion to Rice. "That was a play we really needed," Rice said, "because, before that, you could feel the momentum starting to change." The 49ers held on for a 38-28 win.

The victory earned San Francisco a trip to its fifth Super Bowl (and Rice's third). In Super Bowl XXIX, the 49ers played the San Diego Chargers, a team that San Francisco had crushed 38-15 during the regular season. As expected, the 49ers dominated the game from the start. On their first possession, Young faked a handoff and threw deep over the middle to Rice. Rice split the safeties, caught the ball, and raced into the end zone untouched for a 44-yard touchdown pass. The game was less than two minutes old. The next time the 49ers had the ball, they marched 79 yards in four plays to take a 14-0 lead. The Chargers did manage to cut the lead to 14-7, but their defense could not cope with San Francisco's high-powered offense. At halftime, the score was 28-10, and the Chargers would get no closer for the rest of the game.

When the game finally ended, the 49ers had demolished the Chargers, 49-26, becoming the first team to win five Super Bowls. The combined total score of 75 points and the 10 total touchdowns both remain Super Bowl records (as of 2008).

With 10 catches for 149 yards and three touchdowns in Super Bowl XXIX, Jerry Rice had his third Super Bowl ring. He also moved into first place in all Super Bowl receiving and scoring categories and tied his own record for most touchdown receptions in a Super Bowl. In addition, he did it all with a separated shoulder, suffered in the second quarter. After the game, Young said, "Jerry Rice with one arm is better than everyone in the league with two arms." His performance seemed to clinch his claim to the title, "the best receiver ever."

The Chargers' Stanley Richard *(left)* and Darren Carrington tried in vain to chase down Jerry Rice, who scored a touchdown on this play in Super Bowl XXIX on January 29, 1995. Rice again had three touchdowns in the Super Bowl—this time, though, he was playing with a separated shoulder.

In any other year, Rice would have won the Super Bowl MVP, but that honor went to Steve Young. Young directed the explosive 49er offense that generated seven touchdowns, 28 first downs, and 455 total yards. Young's six touchdown passes also broke the Super Bowl record previously set by former 49ers quarterback Joe Montana. For good measure, Young was the top rusher of the game with 49 rushing yards. "We're part of history," said 49ers guard Jesse Sapolu. "This is probably the best offense people will see in their lifetimes." Steve Young had finally stepped out of Joe Montana's shadow.

THE EBB OF A DYNASTY

The 49ers' run of five Super Bowl wins in 14 seasons (1981–1994) marked them as one of the all-time greatest NFL teams. With that Super Bowl victory, however, the 49ers dynasty began a downward slide. Free agency, age, and poor drafts began to nip away at the team. The 49ers still made the playoffs in the next three years. They were eliminated each time, however, by a new nemesis, Brett Favre and the Green Bay Packers.

Rice somehow managed to have his best statistical season in 1995 even though Young was often injured and the 49ers' running game collapsed. Rice caught a career-high 122 passes for an NFL-record 1,848 receiving yards. Rice also managed to catch 15 touchdown passes, score once on a run, and once on his first career end zone fumble recovery. He even threw a perfect 41-yard touchdown pass. By the end of the year, Rice was the NFL all-time leader in receptions (942, passing Art Monk) and the all-time leader in receiving yards (15,123, passing James Lofton).

"It was one of my best years." Rice recalled in *Go Long*, "but [Green Bay quarterback] Brett Favre was voted the NFL MVP that year over me." Favre had thrown an NFC-record 38 touchdown passes, but Rice was annoyed by the margin of his defeat (69 to 10). "I was really surprised, because . . . I didn't come close," he said in *Rice*. "Not knocking Brett Favre or anything—he had an exceptional year also, and he deserved to win it. But I think people expect me to just go out and do it every year. They don't realize how much time and hard work that I put into it."

The Packers undercut Rice's claim to the MVP by beating the 49ers in the divisional playoffs. Mike Holmgren, Green Bay's coach, had previously been Rice's offensive coordinator at San Francisco. Holmgren based Green Bay's whole game plan around stopping Rice. Double-covered on almost every play, Rice still caught 11 passes for 117 yards, but he gained only 10 yards after his catches and the Packers won, 27-17.

Rice still wanted to play in a fourth Super Bowl, though. Unfortunately for him, the 1996 season was almost a repeat of 1995. The 49ers went 12–4 and Rice recorded 108 receptions for 1,254 yards and eight touchdowns. San Francisco beat Philadelphia in the wild-card playoff game but once again lost to Green Bay in the divisional round. That was enough for George Seifert, who stepped down as head coach to be replaced by Steve Mariucci.

In the three seasons from 1994 to 1996, Rice had a whopping 342 catches for 4,601 yards and 36 touchdowns. He seemed to be getting better with age. Only age finally catches up with everyone. In 1997, Rice's season ended prematurely in the first game of the year. Playing against Tampa Bay, Rice tore the **ligaments** in his left knee. The injury broke his incredible streak of 189 consecutive games played. In 18 seasons of high school, college, and NFL competition, he had never missed a game (except the three strike games). "I take as much pride in the fact that I've never missed a game as I do in any of my records," Rice said.

Rice was out for 14 weeks. He tried to find some humor in the situation by noting that "it wasn't all bad. It gave me some time to work on my golf game, a passion I had picked up 10 years earlier." He also worked hard to recover before the season ended. The 49ers planned to honor Joe Montana against Denver in mid-December, and Rice badly wanted to make it back for that game.

Rice did return, but it was not a good idea. He caught a crucial touchdown pass from Steve Young, but when he came down with the catch, he cracked the **patella** in his left (previously injured) knee even though he was wearing a brace. Without Rice, the 49ers defeated the Minnesota Vikings in the divisional playoffs but lost the NFC Championship Game to the Green Bay Packers 23-10.

Jerry Rice hauled in a pass over Falcons cornerback D.J. Johnson during the first quarter of a game on December 24, 1995. On the play, Rice broke the single-season reception yardage record. He would go on to finish the year with 1,848 receiving yards.

Rice spent the entire off-season working to return his knee to full strength. By the start of the 1998 season, he was healthy and confident. In his comeback season, Rice made a full recovery. He made the Pro Bowl by catching 82 passes for 1,157 yards and nine touchdowns. Rice and Young led the 49ers to a 12–4 record and the team's sixteenth-straight winning season, all with 10 wins or more. In that season, Rice became the oldest player (36) ever to record more than 1,000 receiving yards in a season.

For the fourth straight year, the 49ers faced the Green Bay Packers in the playoffs. In a thrilling game, the 49ers trailed 27-23 in the last seconds. With three seconds left in the game, Young hit Terrell Owens with a 25-yard touchdown pass to win

THE DeBARTOLO FAMILY

The success of the 49ers is linked to their owners, the DeBartolo family. Edward DeBartolo, Sr. (1909–1994) was an entrepreneur who made a fortune developing shopping malls. DeBartolo's company built some of the first enclosed shopping centers in the suburbs after World War II. His brother, Frank DeBartolo, served as his architect. The DeBartolos became fabulously wealthy and branched out into other forms of construction, such as hotels, office parks, and condominiums.

DeBartolo purchased the San Francisco 49ers in 1977 and gave the team to his son, Edward DeBartolo, Jr. (1946–) to run. The DeBartolos used profits from their shopping malls to bankroll the 49ers. Eddie DeBartolo, Jr. made the 49ers the most successful football team of the 1980s. He was one of the most popular owners in the NFL, and most people considered his 49ers to be a "classy" organization. When DeBartolo, Sr. died, his son and daughter (Marie DeBartolo York) inherited the shopping mall empire and the 49ers.

the game for the 49ers, 30-27. The 49ers had finally beaten the Packers. It turned out not to matter, though. A week later, the Atlanta Falcons defeated San Francisco in the divisional playoffs, 20-18.

The 1999 season would be Steve Young's last year. In the third game of the season, Young suffered a concussion, his fourth concussion in three years. Young never made it back and retired at the end of the season. Without their quarterback, the 49ers lost 11 of their last 12 games and finished 4–12. Rice was shocked. This was the team's first losing season since he had

The DeBartolo family's reputation crumbled, however, when Eddie, Jr. was caught in the corruption case of Edwin Edwards, the former governor of Louisiana. DeBartolo, Jr. admitted giving Edwards a $400,000 bribe to try to gain a license for a riverboat casino. In 1998, DeBartolo pleaded guilty to a reduced felony charge in exchange for testifying against Edwards. DeBartolo was fined and suspended from active control of the 49ers for one year. DeBartolo's status as an admitted felon did not hurt his finances; in 2005, his net worth was estimated at $1.4 billion.

DeBartolo returned from his football suspension in 1999, but a series of lawsuits led him to give up his controlling interest in the 49ers to his sister and her husband, John. As of 2007, the York family still controlled the 49ers, but Rice was unimpressed with their leadership. He wrote in *Go Long*, "John York, the current owner, is more interested in marketing and promotional opportunities than he is in bringing top-flight players to San Francisco."

been on the 49ers and only the second time they missed the playoffs in Rice's career. Rice seemed to be slipping, too; he only had 830 receiving yards, the first season he did not reach 1,000 yards since his rookie year.

Young's retirement was the end of an era. He had proven a worthy successor to Joe Montana, and Rice had actually caught more touchdown passes from Young than from Montana. Young did not become the 49ers' starter until his eighth NFL season, and he played a full season only three times during his 15-year career. Yet Young completed 2,667 of 4,149 passes for 33,124 yards and 232 touchdowns with only 107 interceptions. In 2005, Young became the first left-handed quarterback inducted into the Pro Football Hall of Fame.

People often asked Jerry Rice which Hall of Fame quarterback he preferred to play with. Rice always chose Montana: "There was just something special about the way he [Montana] carried himself, his leadership, and his abilities as quarterback," Rice said in *Go Long*. "Taking nothing away from Steve, of course, who proved that he is among the NFL's best, but if I had a choice of quarterbacks to be behind center in a big game, there would be no question it would be Joe."

Practice and Timing

Jerry Rice had one simple explanation for how he was able to maintain his level of excellence for so long. He wrote, in *Go Long*, "How you practice = How you play. It's that simple. I don't care if we're talking about basketball or ballet, cooking or checkers. The way in which you prepare for a challenge is usually related to your success in the same challenge."

Even back in college, Rice's emphasis on practice was already apparent. Willie Totten, his college quarterback, said, "He wasn't that fast, but he worked real hard. If you were the fastest guy on the team, he wanted to race you. He lost a lot of races. But he ran the best routes and was the hardest worker on the team."

As early as Rice's first year at Mississippi Valley State, he noticed the varying degrees of work ethic on a team. "There were some guys who gave 100 percent every day in practice," he remembered, "and others who exerted just enough effort to get by. . . . I couldn't understand how anybody could *not* give an all-out effort daily."

Rice's work ethic as a professional was legendary, but in the first few years of his career, he seemed to worry as much about how he looked. He drove fancy cars with personalized license plates. In 1987, his Afro hairstyle was so high that his teammates nicknamed him "Fifi" (like a poodle) or "6'7" (as in 6'2" with 5 inches of hair). Rice later said, "That was me trying to fit in. . . . You're always looking for something different, so people can relate to you."

Rice was worried that the media and fans would not notice him among the older 49ers stars like Joe Montana, Roger Craig, Dwight Clark, and Ronnie Lott. So Rice began to celebrate his touchdowns by doing a "Cabbage Patch" dance. It was funny but not exactly dignified. In time, the professionalism of Montana and Craig began to wear off on him. "So many players had their celebrations and signature moves, and I wanted to put my own stamp on the game," Rice said in *Go Long*. "But I was stupid. . . . Why not just hand the football to the referee? Joe and Roger were the consummate pros, and they didn't need to show off, so why should I? To be a professional means to act like a professional. . . . I haven't showboated during a TD celebration since."

TOUGH TRAINING

In 1989, Rice began to train with Roger Craig, trainer Ray Farris, and a few other football players in San Carlos, south of San Francisco. Craig was famous for his brutal workouts and his commitment to hard work. There was a running track at San Carlos they could use in addition to some great running hills with beautiful scenery. Almost daily in the spring and early summer, the group would meet for grueling

Jerry Rice ran wind sprints alone before the first practice of the 49ers training camp in 1997. In 1989, Rice began to train in the off-season with teammate Roger Craig, who was known for his grueling workouts.

workouts at 7:30 A.M. Rice's normal off-season workout day lasted until noon.

Three times a week the group would run up the 2.5-mile (4-kilometer) hill against the clock. In *Go Long*, Rice said, "If you couldn't endure the pain . . . the hill wasn't for you. I was in such good condition from running the hill that during the season, there was little difference in my play from the start of the game until the final whistle." One Dallas cornerback confirmed Rice's judgment. He said, "What a lot of guys don't understand about Jerry is that with him, football's a 12-month thing. When other people slow down in the eighth or ninth game, he picks it up. He separates himself from the others because of his stamina. He's a natural, but he still works. That's what separates the good from the great."

On days they did not run the big hill, Rice and his teammates would work on speed repetitions at the track. They would mix short distance runs and sprints under the early morning sun. After all his conditioning workouts, Rice would go to the gym to lift weights for another two hours. Three days a week, he would work on his upper body and three days a week, he would work on his lower body.

Rice, Craig, and a few friends ran the same program every off-season in San Carlos. Word quickly spread. Many 49ers joined Rice as did friends from other teams who wanted to be in top shape for the season. On average, 15 players might be

EXERCISE REGIMEN

On Jerry Rice's Web site (http://www.jerryricefootball.com), there is a section called "Jerry's Gym." The section lists various exercises for legs, back, chest, biceps, triceps, and shoulders, and offers different routines. Here's a sampling:

For the legs, Routine 3 suggests angled leg presses, calf presses, leg extensions, and lying leg curls.

For the chest, Routine 1 lists the incline bench press (dumbbells or barbells), the bench press (dumbbells or barbells), the decline press (dumbbells or barbells), parallel-bar dips, and flat bench dumbbell flies.

For the triceps, Routine 3 suggests one-arm dumbbell kickbacks, one-arm dumbbell extensions, and one-dumbbell triceps extensions.

More than 20 routines can be found on the "Jerry's Gym" page.

training on a given day, peaking in late June just before training camp opened. Some were famous and some were not, but all shared a desire to be in the best possible shape when the football season began.

Rice had to work hard because his time of 4.6 in the 40-yard dash probably put him in the bottom half of wide receivers. However, as Rice noted in *Go Long*, "There's a big difference between being fast and having football speed. Football speed is how crisp you come out of running routes, how quickly you can stop on a dime and change direction, and how quickly you break the line of scrimmage when the ball is snapped." Rice believed that a player could learn football speed through hard work on the track and in the weight room. It certainly worked for him, as he seemed to get faster as the years passed.

The quarterback/receiver relationship was another element of the game that Rice felt could be developed through hard work. "You've got to have that chemistry, man," Rice said, "and I had it with Montana. And then after Montana left, I had to develop that with Steve Young and it's all about practice."

Of course, not every football player worked hard in the off-season. Some players did absolutely nothing in the spring and waited until training camp to get into shape. Rice was always amazed by his receiving partner, John Taylor. Taylor refused to train in the off-season but still managed to be one of the best receivers in the NFL. Taylor commented, "He [Rice] worked hard, and I was the opposite." To Rice, practice was almost religious in nature. For Taylor, it was just boring.

Rice, like many football players, was a big believer in poring over videotape to look for weaknesses in his opponents. Mike Shanahan, the Broncos coach and former 49er offensive coordinator, noted that "Jerry worked on running routes, coming out of breaks. He studied. He'd take the top 10 guys from the AFC, the top 10 guys from the NFC, and he'd go back and forth with the tape, study each guy and see why they were successful. He studied their moves, their techniques and how they ran different routes." Rice's drive for perfection took in almost every aspect of preparation and practice.

In addition to Rice's addiction to practice, he also kept up his concern for appearance. In *Go Long*, he said, "Ever since high school, I had thought that presentation and style were everything. I've never understood how someone could dress sloppily and not care about how they look."

Some players and writers made fun of Rice's desire for a perfectly tailored uniform every week for nearly 20 years. In fact, Rice's appearance was so important to him that he often changed to a clean uniform at halftime. Before he ran out on the field, he would make sure to shine his helmet and put on brand new shoes. In Oakland, the staff had to lay out four or five pairs of socks for Rice because they had to fit perfectly. Rice made no apologies. "The way I prepare and the way I look," Rice declared, "are the most important parts of my performance. It's part of having the right attitude."

RULE CHANGES

Some elements of football are beyond attitude and practice. Had Rice played football 20 years earlier, his career would have looked very different. Rice's statistics greatly benefited from sweeping changes in the NFL rules to add action and scoring to football games. No amount of hard work by Rice could have taken into account rule changes that allowed for more passing in professional football.

In the late 1970s, the Pittsburgh Steelers had dominated the NFL, winning four titles behind their intimidating "Steel Curtain" defense. In the 1975 Super Bowl, the Steelers' defense limited the Minnesota Vikings to just 17 rushing yards in a 16-6 victory. In the last nine games of the 1976 season, the Steelers gave up a ridiculous 28 total points. In 1978, the Steelers held their opponents to an NFL-low 195 points and won their third Super Bowl.

The Steelers had two sublime wide receivers in John Stallworth and Lynn Swann. Both were incredibly clutch in Pittsburgh's Super Bowl victories, and both made the Hall of Fame. Rice idolized them when he watched them on television. Yet Stallworth caught only 537 passes in 14 seasons and Swann only 336 in his nine-year career.

The NFL was worried. Scoring was at the lowest point in football's post-World War II history. The NFL knew that Americans liked offense; many U.S. sports fans disliked soccer, mainly because there was not enough scoring. Football's share of the television audience concerned team owners far more than the traditions of the game or the people who went to see the sport in person. Everyone knew that defense usually won championships; the Steelers had demonstrated it yet again. Defense, though, did not bring in casual television viewers who would buy the advertised products. The NFL was determined to surpass baseball as America's sport and make vast amounts of money in television contracts. To do that, the league needed to make it harder to play defense and easier to score. In other words, the NFL needed to change the rules to make it easier to throw the ball.

Football was not unique in this strategy. Basketball had reacted to the chants of "Defense" by Knick fans in Madison Square Garden by reinstating the dunk and featuring Michael Jordan as the face of the league. Baseball had reacted to pitchers' superiority in the 1960s by altering its rules to help hitters. The NHL was about to shift into the high-scoring Gretzky years of the 1980s. Americans wanted to see home runs and slap shots, not hit-and-runs and clever skating.

For example, in football in the early 1970s, a cornerback could hit a wide receiver at any point on the field. Many wide receivers could not handle that kind of pounding. In 1977, the NFL changed the rules so that defenders could make contact with eligible receivers only once within five yards of the line of scrimmage.

Jerry Rice and Cowboys cornerback Deion Sanders tangled during a game in 1995. Because of a rule change in the late 1970s, defenders are only allowed to hit a receiver once within five yards of the line of scrimmage. The NFL made several rule changes to boost scoring in games.

In the same year, the league made it illegal for a defensive lineman to strike an opponent above the shoulders or to use a head slap. Before that rule, defensive linemen would just go punching left-right-left into the backfield. Now offensive line-men would not have to tuck their heads and duck when they were pass blocking.

In 1979, the NFL passed a rule change to protect quarter-backs. Quarterbacks were usually the most marketable and famous people on a football team. Television viewers did not want to see the stars lost to injury and then have to watch third-string quarterbacks play. Therefore, the league ruled that the referee should whistle the play dead once a quarterback was clearly in the grasp of a tackler. This ensured that the marquee quarterbacks were not pulverized.

The changes in the late 1970s worked. By Rice's rookie year, a CBS Sports/New York Times survey reported that 53 percent of the nation's sports fans said they most enjoyed watching football compared with 18 percent for baseball. In 1984, teams averaged 42.4 points per game, the second-highest total since the 1970 merger. Lynn Swann never caught more than 61 passes in a single season. Amazingly, Jerry Rice caught more than 61 passes *every year* of his career except his first, his last, and the year he was injured. He was the right man playing in the right time.

Rule changes or not, Rice still had to take advantage of the opportunity. His famously brutal workout regimen seemed almost to stop the advancement of age. In addition, Rice's fear of failure ensured that he remained driven no matter how much he accomplished. As he said in *Go Long*, "Fear of failure isn't always a bad thing. It helped keep me focused on the task. And a fear of failure has carried me through my life."

Two of Rice's former offensive coordinators became Super Bowl-winning coaches with other teams. Even then, however, they could not hide their admiration for Jerry Rice. Mike Shanahan noted that Rice left "no stone unturned in his prepa-ration. Every time he hits the practice field, he's like a rookie trying to make the team. He practices the same way during the first week of the season as he does before the Super Bowl, and those work habits carry over to the rest of the team." Mike Holmgren's evaluation was even simpler: "I can't think of another player that more exemplifies the drive, work habits, and commitment it takes to reach the top."

"I'm old school," Rice declared. "If you want to get better, put in the hard work and sweat. There is no substitute for hard work."

Last Hurrah (2000–2004)

By 1999, Jerry Rice could sense that his years with the 49ers were coming to a close. The local sportswriters declared that Rice was not the player he once was. Rice noticed that the team was drafting young wide receivers like J.J. Stokes and Terrell Owens. Many fans suggested that the 49ers trade Rice so that the younger receivers could develop. San Francisco was no longer a Super Bowl contender. In 1999, the 49ers were a dismal 4–12. In 2000, they improved only slightly to 6–10. Rice's contract was extremely large, and the team wanted to spend the money on younger players.

Bill Walsh was now the general manager of the 49ers and made all the personnel decisions. Walsh and Rice had always been very close, but Walsh was not sentimental when it came to business. The 49ers were notorious for cutting formerly great players before they were ready to retire. Before the 2000 season, Walsh supposedly told Rice, "It's time for you to move on."

Rice noted, "It doesn't matter how good you are or what your loyalty is to a team. Professional football is a business, and you will be replaced. I saw it up close when Roger Craig, Ronnie Lott, and Joe Montana departed. . . . It was a business back when I broke in, and it has grown tenfold since." Walsh decided that he could not afford to keep the aging Rice and his $2.5 million salary. Rice was annoyed: "I thought I could still contribute in a big way and that they could have found a way to make things work."

Rice's last home game for the 49ers in 2000 was against the Chicago Bears. Rice caught seven passes, but Terrell Owens caught 20, an NFL single-game record (that still stands as of 2008). The wide receiver's torch seemed to have been passed, at least at the 49ers.

A MOVE ACROSS THE BAY

Yet Rice did not want to retire. He believed he still had several good years left. He began to shop around for a new team. Jon Gruden, the Oakland Raiders' coach since 1998, had once been an assistant coach with the 49ers. Gruden knew Rice and believed he had a few years left. For Rice, the Raiders offered him the best shot at winning another Super Bowl ring. It also allowed him to stay in his newly built 9,000-square-foot home in the Bay Area. After 16 seasons as a 49er, Rice left the team to sign with the Raiders in June 2001.

Of course, it was not quite that simple. The Oakland Raiders were the hated cross-bay rivals of the 49ers. For fans in San Francisco, Rice's appearance in Oakland's silver and black uniform seemed an action bordering on treason. Others interpreted it as a way to stick it to the 49ers. Rice himself said in *Go Long* that he "had another motivation: proving my old employer wrong. . . . An athlete enjoys nothing better than showing up a team that gave up on him, and I felt the same way.

Jerry Rice's teammates carried him off the field on December 17, 2000, after the 49ers beat the Chicago Bears 17-0. It was thought that the game could be Rice's last home game as a 49er, and it turned out it was. In June 2001, he signed with the Oakland Raiders after he was released by San Francisco.

The 49ers believed I was ready to be put out to pasture, but I believed otherwise."

In 2000, Oakland's passing game had ranked a mediocre fifteenth in the NFL; the team hoped Rice's arrival would boost the aerial attack. In Oakland, Rice had to play **split end** rather than **flanker**. He lined up on the line of scrimmage instead of behind it. This meant increased contact with cornerbacks. At first, Rice had trouble learning the new offensive system. Gruden and Rice, both strong-willed, clashed over specific plays and receiver routes. Of Gruden, Rice said, "He was crazy, and still is, but I love the man."

Under Gruden, Oakland was a team on the rise. He had seen something no one else had noticed in Rich Gannon, a longtime journeyman quarterback with unusual mobility. Gruden signed Gannon in 1999 (when Gannon was 34) and based the Raiders' offense around him. Soon, both the quarterback and the team flourished. The Raiders posted an 8–8 season in 1999, equal to their record of a year before. Then they finished 12–4 in 2000, the team's most successful season in a decade. They made it to the AFC Championship

MR. RAIDER

Oakland's other offensive star besides Rich Gannon and Jerry Rice was wide receiver Tim Brown. At Notre Dame in 1987, Brown became the first wide receiver ever to win the Heisman Trophy. For years, Brown had been the Raiders' only real receiving threat in addition to being a superb punt and kick returner. In 2000, he scored a career-best 11 touchdowns and led the team in receptions for the ninth straight year. As the team's superstar, he had never had to share the stage with anyone, especially someone with the star power of Rice.

Everyone wondered if Rice and Brown could play together on the same team. Both were used to being the unquestioned primary receiver. In an article in *Pro Football Weekly*, Gruden said, "Everybody keeps asking me about Tim Brown and Jerry Rice. ... This is getting a little ridiculous. They're getting along just fine." In *Go Long*, Rice said, "I never had a problem sharing passes with Tim. Honestly, I was honored to be on the field with

Game, losing 16-3 to the eventual Super Bowl champion Baltimore Ravens.

THRIVING AS A RAIDER

Rice turned out to be a brilliant acquisition by the Oakland Raiders. In 2000, Rice's last season at San Francisco, he caught 75 passes for 805 yards and seven touchdowns. For the Raiders in 2001, Rice caught 83 passes for 1,139 yards and nine touchdowns. In his autobiography, Rice wrote in italics, *"Take that, San Francisco."* The Raiders finished 10–6 and won their second straight AFC West title.

him. At that point in our careers, we had already established ourselves. ... Tim displayed grace and class and understood that the team was above all else."

When Brown retired in 2004, he had 14,934 receiving yards, second only to Rice in NFL history. He also had 1,094 receptions (ranked third all-time), 100 career touchdown catches (sixth), and 19,682 combined net yards (fifth). He caught at least one pass in 179 consecutive games, the third-longest streak in NFL history behind Art Monk's 183 and Rice's 274.

Perhaps more important, he was a huge fan favorite in Oakland and was admired by many Raiders players and staff for the 15 years he spent with the team. Marcus Allen, a Hall of Fame running back for the Raiders, said in the *San Francisco Chronicle* that Brown was "one of the finest human beings that I've ever met. And one of the finest football players I've ever met, too." In fact, Tim Brown was so associated with the team, he was sometimes simply known as "Mr. Raider."

In their first playoff game, the Raiders defeated the New York Jets 38-24. The Raiders offense was in high gear, outgaining the Jets in total yards, 502 to 410. Quarterback Rich Gannon was 23 of 29 for 294 yards and two touchdowns. However, it was Rice's performance that really caught the eye. The 39-year-old wide receiver more than repaid his salary by catching nine passes for 183 yards (an exceptional 20.3 yard-per-reception average), including a 21-yard touchdown in the fourth quarter. His nine receptions tied a Raider playoff record.

Unfortunately for Rice, the Raiders lost their next playoff game to the New England Patriots. Although the game was played in a snowstorm, Rice still managed to catch four passes for 48 yards. The game, known as the "Tuck Rule Game," ended in bitter controversy. Late in the fourth quarter, the Raiders recovered an apparent fumble by Patriots quarterback Tom Brady. The fumble recovery would have resulted in a Raiders victory. However, the referees reviewed the play on instant replay and declared it an incomplete pass. They ruled that Brady had pump-faked and had not yet "tucked" the ball into his body. According to the rules, this cannot result in a fumble. The Patriots kept possession of the ball, and in the wind and snow, Adam Vinatieri kicked a line-drive 45-yard field goal with 27 seconds left to tie the score. The game went into overtime; the Patriots won the coin toss and drove 61 yards in 15 plays. Vinatieri kicked a 23-yard field goal and the Patriots won 16-13. Oakland never saw the ball in overtime. Three weeks later, New England beat the St. Louis Rams to win Super Bowl XXXVI.

Gruden's 40–28 record with the Raiders was not good enough for Oakland's owner, the legendary Al Davis. He thought that Gruden was not the best coach for the team. Davis decided to trade the rights to the coach to the Tampa Bay Buccaneers in exchange for four draft choices and $8 million. The price was high, but Tampa Bay thought it was worth it. It turned out to be a brilliant move for the Buccaneers.

ON TO ANOTHER SUPER BOWL

To replace Gruden, Oakland hired Bill Callahan, who had spent the last four seasons as the Raiders' offensive coordinator and had a reputation as one of the best offensive coaches in the NFL. In 2002, under Callahan's guidance, the Raiders led the NFL in total passing yards (4,689) for the first time in team history. Behind this potent offense, the Raiders tied for the AFC's best record at 11–5. Rich Gannon won the NFL Most Valuable Player Award, completing 418 out of 618 passes for 4,689 yards, 26 touchdowns, and only 10 interceptions. His 418 completions was an NFL record at the time (Drew Brees broke the completion record in 2007).

Rice's season was almost as remarkable as Gannon's. Rice made the Pro Bowl for the thirteenth (and last) time in his career with 92 receptions for 1,211 yards and seven touchdowns. In *Go Long*, Rice said, "For much of my career, Joe Montana or Steve Young was behind center. Now, it was Rich Gannon's turn. We never quite had the same chemistry that Joe and I had, but we managed to find our groove. Rich had an awkward sidearm throwing motion, which was hard to read, but somehow he got the football where he wanted it to go."

All of Oakland's receivers benefited from the improved offense. Tim Brown had 81 receptions for 930 yards and two touchdowns while Jerry Porter had 51 receptions for 688 yards and nine touchdowns. Charlie Garner, the team's leading rusher, also led all NFL running backs in receiving with 91 receptions for 941 yards and another four touchdowns.

In the divisional round of the playoffs, Oakland defeated the New York Jets 30-10. Oakland pulled away from a 10-10 halftime tie by forcing four turnovers. Rice finished with four receptions for 47 yards and a touchdown. Callahan's offense also worked spectacularly well in the AFC Championship Game against the Tennessee Titans. As a surprise, Oakland called only one running play in the first three quarters of the game. Instead, the Raiders relied on the passing of the

37-year-old Gannon. The strategy worked, as Gannon threw for 286 passing yards and three touchdowns. Rice had five receptions for 79 yards and the Raiders won 41-24.

The victory put the Raiders into Super Bowl XXXVII against none other than the Tampa Bay Buccaneers, coached by ex-Raider coach Jon Gruden. For most of their history, the Buccaneers had trouble winning games. The team only made the playoffs three times in their first 20 seasons. That changed when the team hired Tony Dungy as its head coach in 1996. Dungy put together one of the best defenses in the NFL and guided the Buccaneers to four playoff appearances in his six years as head coach. The team's weak offense, however, was a major factor in their playoff losses. The Buccaneers had hired Gruden to fix the offense.

The Raiders entered the game favored to win their first Super Bowl in 19 years. Most of the pregame media speculation revolved around Gruden. Did he have any idea of Oakland's game plan? If he did, how would this affect the game? As it turned out, Gruden's knowledge of the Raiders' offense was a major factor in the Buccaneers' victory. Almost all of the plays run by Oakland's offense were plays that Gruden specifically told Tampa Bay's defense to look for. Even more amazingly, Oakland had not changed the **audible** signals that Gruden himself had installed. This meant that the Buccaneers knew all of the Raiders' audibles. Partially as a result, Tampa Bay completely dominated Oakland in Super Bowl XXXVII, outgaining the Raiders in total yards (365 to 269), rushing yards (150 to 19), and first downs (24 to 11).

The score was still tied 3-3 going into the second quarter, but then the Buccaneers scored 17 points to lead 20-3 at half-time. Oakland never got close again. Tampa Bay dominated the game for most of the third quarter and at one point led 34-3. At the end of the game, Oakland finally managed to move the ball and make the score respectable. With six minutes left, Gannon threw a 48-yard touchdown pass to Rice to cut the

Looking ahead toward the end zone, Jerry Rice outgunned Tampa Bay defender Nate Webster to score a 48-yard touchdown in the fourth quarter of Super Bowl XXXVII. The touchdown was not enough as the Bucs won 48-21 over the Raiders.

Raiders deficit to 34-21. But Tampa Bay intercepted two passes and returned them both for touchdowns. The Buccaneers won 48-21, their first title in team history.

Gannon, who had only been intercepted 10 times all year, threw a Super Bowl-record five interceptions, three of which were returned for touchdowns. Rice was the Raiders' leading receiver with five catches for 77 yards and a touchdown. With his touchdown reception, Rice became the first player ever to catch a touchdown pass in four Super Bowls. This was a nice personal accomplishment but did not ease the pain of the defeat. "Of course, I took the loss hard," Rice remembered. "Sitting on the edge of the bed, replaying the game in my mind . . . it really hit me that we had lost. Tears began to roll down my cheeks. . . . That loss stays with me." Super Bowl XXXVII was the final Super Bowl game Rice would play in (and the only one he lost).

A TEAM'S SWIFT DECLINE

If the Raiders thought they would be returning to the Super Bowl the next year, they were mistaken. Oakland dropped from 11–5 in 2002 to 4–12 in 2003. The aging offense disintegrated, going from second in the NFL in 2002 to the bottom five in the following season. After the team got off to a poor start, several players publicly blamed the coach. Most observers agreed that Callahan lost control of the team. After the season ended, the Raiders fired Callahan. He was replaced by Norv Turner, who turned out to be no more successful in his two-year stint.

For Rice, the 2003 season was particularly frustrating. He had just two touchdowns for the entire year, the lowest total in his career (except for his two-game 1997 season). He also did not like his role. Coming off a 92-catch Pro Bowl year, Rice felt he could still excel in the NFL. He complained that the Raiders wanted him "to be more of a mentor to the younger guys, not a playing contributor. I had no problems teaching younger players, but I still felt I could be a presence on the field."

In 2004, the Raiders only managed a 5–11 record, but Rice was not at Oakland to see the end of the season. He grew

A dejected Jerry Rice stared at his feet in the final minutes of the Raiders-Bills game on September 19, 2004. Rice did not have a catch in the game, ending his streak of 274 games with at least one reception.

frustrated with his small role in Norv Turner's offense. When his record streak of games with at least one catch was about to end at 274 (in the second week), Rice threw his helmet to the ground in disgust; only one pass was thrown in his direction the entire game. The last time Rice did not catch a pass was on December 1, 1985. Yet Rice went without a catch in two other games under Turner.

OFF TO SEATTLE

After the Raiders lost to the Denver Broncos 31-3, Rice felt the time was right to move on. As he said in *Go Long*, "I wasn't ready to quit playing just yet and with things in decline in Oakland, I wanted out." Rice asked the Raiders to trade him if they were not going to play him. The Raiders responded by sending him to the Seattle Seahawks in October for a seventh-round draft pick, "not exactly ego-enhancing," as Rice remembered. When he left Oakland, Rice had only five receptions for 67 yards and no touchdowns.

Many football fans believed it was time for Rice to retire. Rice recalled, "Some believed I would tarnish my legacy by continuing to play while others thought *how sad* for Jerry Rice—he just doesn't know when to quit. But you have to create your own destiny. I wasn't going to let anybody but me decide when it was time to retire."

In public, at least, Rice refused to believe that his skills had eroded in any way. He was now in his twentieth NFL season, but he told the Seattle media, "I'm 42, but I feel like I'm 28. I really don't see a difference. I think I'm capable of doing what I did 20 years ago. I just have to have an opportunity."

In Seattle, Rice was reunited with coach Mike Holmgren. Holmgren had won a Super Bowl with Green Bay, but before that, he had been Rice's offensive coordinator with the 49ers from 1989 to 1991. Holmgren insisted that Rice would see meaningful playing time for the Seahawks. Holmgren said, "Do I expect him to produce? Yes, I do." If nothing else, Holmgren expected Rice's workout habits to rub off on his teammates. Rice said: "I don't have to come in here and be the No. 1 guy. I just want to contribute."

As he had for 20 years, Rice wore No. 80 when he joined Seattle. This was not as simple as it seemed. From 1976 to 1989, the number had belonged to Steve Largent, Seattle's Hall of Fame receiver. In 1995, Seattle had retired the number in honor of Largent. Rice received special permission from Largent to wear No 80 during his time in Seattle. It helped that Largent was always one of Rice's favorite receivers. Largent "had such heart, such determination, and I respected that," Rice said in *Go Long*. "He wasn't big, he wasn't fast, but he ran great receiving routes and made the catches."

The Seahawks had been a preseason pick to make it to the Super Bowl in 2004. Instead, the team was struggling even to make the playoffs. Seattle started the season 3–0 but won only six of its remaining 13 games. The team's inconsistent play frustrated fans, and the acquisition of Rice was supposed to help steady the team. Rice played in 11 games for Seattle, catching 25 passes for 362 yards and three touchdowns, including a 56-yard reception. The Seahawks just managed to win the NFC West with a 9–7 record.

In the 2004 playoffs, the Seahawks faced the St. Louis Rams. Although the Rams barely made the playoffs with an 8–8 record, two of their regular-season wins were against Seattle. With the Rams leading 27-20 at the end of the playoff game, the Seahawks drove for a game-tying touchdown. On fourth and goal from the Rams' 5-yard line, Seattle quarterback Matt Hasselbeck's pass slipped through a receiver's hands in the end zone. The Rams held on to beat the Seahawks for the third time. Hasselback completed 27 passes in the game; Darrell Jackson caught 12 of them. Jerry Rice, one of the greatest receivers of all time, had no receptions at all.

After the game, Rice said, "I still feel like I have football left in me, a lot of football in me." However, he was wrong. The playoff loss to the Rams would be his last NFL game.

This is
My Life...

Jerry Rice's brief stay in Seattle had not been particularly successful. He missed his family, who had remained in the San Francisco Bay area. The wet weather in Seattle did not agree with him. **Tendonitis** in his left heel constantly bothered him. Could he really make it through another season at age 42? Thoughts of retirement began to creep into Rice's head.

He decided, however, to give it one more try and told his agent to find him another team. The Denver Broncos decided to take a shot. Denver coach Mike Shanahan had been Rice's offensive coordinator for three years at San Francisco in the early 1990s. Shanahan thought Rice might have one more season left in him.

So in July 2005, Rice suited up in his fourth different uniform and took part in yet another preseason training camp.

Jerry Rice studied plays on July 30, 2005, during training camp with the Denver Broncos. Rice hoped that he would come out of preseason as the Broncos' third receiver. When he was told he would be no higher than fourth on the depth chart, Rice decided it was time to retire.

Rice's goal was to be one of the top three receivers at Denver and have a chance at one more Super Bowl. At the end of the preseason, though, he had only four catches for 24 yards. Shanahan called Rice into his office and told him he would be no higher than the fourth receiver on the depth chart. After a brilliant 20-year career, Rice did not want to be the fourth or fifth receiver for the Broncos. He said, "I knew it was time. I didn't want to start over anywhere else."

On September 5, 2005, Rice held a news conference in Denver. With tears in his eyes, Rice formally announced his retirement from the NFL. "This is a happy day," Rice said at the conference. "I think the tears that you see basically is that I have really enjoyed this ride. I'm done. I'm looking forward to the next phase of my life."

The truth was that Rice was not sure what the "next phase" of his life should be. For a short time, he enjoyed an aimless life of playing golf and watching football games on television. Then he grew bored with it. Yet he noted in *Go Long*, "Aside from family, football was all I ever knew. It was all I had done since I was 15 years old. I lived it, breathed it, loved it—so much so that I forgot to take a look at the bigger picture. What am I going to do now? . . . What can I do to fill the void in my life? . . . At 44 years old, I still had a lot of life to live."

One of Rice's interests was charity work. Earlier in his career, Rice had founded the 127 Foundation (named for his NFL-record 127th career touchdown) to organize his charitable donations. Rice's 127 Foundation supported causes such as the United Negro College Fund, Mississippi Valley State, Packard Children's Hospital at Stanford University, Big Brothers/Big Sisters, AIDS research, and the Bay Area Omega Boys Club.

Rice did more than just give money; he took an active role in fundraising. Each year, he would organize and play in golf tournaments to raise money for his foundation. Rice often appeared at the March of Dimes Walk in San Francisco, leading calisthenics, signing autographs, and making motivational speeches. With three children of his own—Jaqui Bonet (born 1987), Jerry, Jr. (born 1991), and Jada Symone (born 1996)—Rice reasoned, "Jerry, your kids are healthy, but there are those out there who aren't. So why not do whatever you can to help?" But charity work did not offer enough of a competitive rush for Rice. Then he found something that perfectly matched his desire to stay in front of the public with his competitive streak.

HOW THE MIGHTY HAVE FALLEN

The years from 2003 to 2007 have not been good for the San Francisco 49ers or the Oakland Raiders. Certainly Jerry Rice was not the only reason for the success of both teams. However, it is ironic how far both teams have fallen since Rice left.

The period since the 2002 season has been a disaster for San Francisco. The 49ers have missed the playoffs every year and have not won more than seven games in any season. They traded Terrell Owens, their exciting wide receiver, to the Philadelphia Eagles after the 2003 season, even though he scored 83 touchdowns in eight seasons with the 49ers.

The lowest point for San Francisco probably occurred during the 2004 season when the Seattle Seahawks shut out the 49ers 34-0. It was the first time the 49ers had been shut out in 420 regular-season and 36 playoff games, an NFL record. The last shutout had been an amazing 27 years before when they were defeated 7-0 by the Atlanta Falcons in 1977, eight years before Rice joined the team.

The Oakland Raiders have been even worse than the 49ers. Since 2002, when Bill Callahan led the Raiders to the Super Bowl, they have not won more then five games in any season. During that stretch, the Raiders have gone 19–61 (.238), the worst record in professional football. Which team is second-worst?—none other than the 49ers with a 25–55 record (.313). Rice's verdict in 2007: "As for the San Francisco 49ers, I don't see a bright future the way things are going now."

JERRY DANCES

By 2005, reality shows like *Survivor* and *American Idol* had been dominating American television for about five years. These shows had consistently garnered huge television audiences (and profits) and spawned a host of knockoffs. One of the surprise reality shows of the 2004–2005 television season was a program entitled *Dancing with the Stars*. It was this television show that caught Rice's attention.

The idea of the show was that pairs of dancers, made up of a celebrity dancer and a professional, competed on a weekly basis to be crowned champion. The professional dancer had to teach the celebrity how to perform specific dances. The duo would then perform live on the show each week. The dancers were scored by a panel of three professional ballroom judges as well as viewers of the program (by phone, text message, or the Internet). The couple who received the lowest total score each week was eliminated until only one pair remained.

Rice did not initially want to participate on a dancing show. He had never really danced in his life. His agent, however, thought that an appearance by Rice on *Dancing with the Stars* might be a way to break into major television work. Rice was terrified of embarrassing himself but could not resist the strangeness of the challenge. He said in *Go Long*, "I had never shied away from difficult tasks in the past. Yes, my image was important to me but since when did I let others dictate what I would do with my life? . . . I knew that I had to take risks and get out of my comfort zone."

So during the 2005–2006 television season, Rice was paired with dancer Anna Trebunskaya on *Dancing with the Stars*. The two of them practiced for hours each day for weeks at a time. Rice's amazing work ethic came in handy once again, and his obvious determination made him a favorite with both judges and viewers. To Rice's great surprise, he achieved amazing success and popularity on the show. People

With a bit of flair, Jerry Rice and his daughter Jada arrived at the world premiere of the movie *Pirates of the Caribbean: Dead Man's Chest* held on June 24, 2006, at Disneyland in Anaheim, California. Rice's appearance on the TV show *Dancing with the Stars* opened up new opportunities for him.

who would not know a cornerback from a quarterback suddenly became new fans of Jerry Rice.

More than 18 million viewers tuned in to see the final dance competition in February 2006, and another 15 million watched the announcement of the results three days later. Rice and Trebunskaya reached the final two before finally losing to singer Drew Lachey and his partner Cheryl Burke.

Rice's competitive streak was no less evident in dancing than in football. He complained that "finishing second stunk, especially after all we had put into the show. It was like losing the Super Bowl. . . . I was hurt, sad, and believed that we'd deserved to win the competition." Yet Rice loved his first major venture into the world of entertainment. In *Go Long*, he said, "When I look back on the *Dancing with the Stars* experience, I have no regrets. Millions of Americans got to see a totally different side of me."

As his agent predicted, *Dancing with the Stars* opened some doors for Rice in television, movies, and radio. It also whetted Rice's appetite to do more of that sort of work. He began to co-host a sports show in the San Francisco area as well as a talk show on Sirius Satellite Radio's NFL radio channel. "Twenty years ago I was too shy to even think about a job on television," he said, "but now, it's what I want to do."

One casualty of Rice's retirement seemed to be his marriage. In June 2007, Jackie Rice filed papers in family court to dissolve the couple's marriage. The specific reasons for the request were not revealed at the time. Her attorney said, "When the parties are ready to talk about it, they will." Jerry Rice made only a brief statement: "I am saddened to announce that Jackie and I have separated after 20 years of marriage. Our main priority is the well-being of our children, and we ask that you please respect our family's privacy during this difficult time." Meanwhile, the couple put their Bay Area estate up for sale for a reported $22 million.

LIVING LIFE TO THE FULLEST

What the future will hold for Rice is unclear. However, he made it clear that a passive life of golf and television viewing was not his ultimate goal: "This is my life and I'm going to live it to the fullest and enjoy every moment. I am going to continue to try new things even when others tell me not to. I am going to put myself and my reputation on the line seeking out my passions."

Regardless of what Rice chooses to do, it is unlikely that his second career will measure up to his first in the NFL. Rice's football statistics are so overwhelming that they defy belief. As of 2007, Rice's 1,549 career receptions are 448 catches ahead of the second-place mark held by Cris Carter. His 22,895 career receiving yards are an astonishing 7,961 yards ahead of the second-place spot held by Tim Brown, his old teammate on the Raiders. Rice's 197 touchdown receptions are 67 scores more than Carter's 130, and his 208 total touchdowns were 33 scores ahead of running back Emmitt Smith. These staggering records look as if they may last for a long time.

Perhaps the most amazing aspect of Rice's career was his incredible consistency. He averaged 77 catches a season for *20 years*! He caught passes in a mind-boggling 274 consecutive games. Rice had 17 seasons with at least 50 receptions and 14 seasons with at least 1,000 receiving yards—both NFL records.

Rice's longevity also seemed otherworldly. In his 20 NFL seasons, Rice missed only 17 regular-season games, 14 of them in a single year (1997) when he tore his knee ligaments and the other three in the strike-shortened season of 1987. His 303 games are by far the most ever played by an NFL wide receiver. (Tim Brown is second with 255; no active receiver has more than 200). Rice's career lasted so long he made the NFL All-Decade Team in both the 1980s and the 1990s.

Rice was also extremely clutch. He holds the Super Bowl records for receptions (33), yards receiving (589), touchdown receptions (8), points scored (48), receptions in a single game (11), and yards receiving in a single game (215). Rice has caught eight touchdown passes in the Super Bowl; his nearest competitors have three. No doubt, he will be elected to the Pro Football Hall of Fame in 2010, the first year he becomes eligible.

Perhaps Rice summed up his career best at the press conference when he retired. "I play the game with a lot of determination, a lot of poise, a lot of pride," Rice said. "I think what you saw on the field was an individual who really loved the game. . . . I enjoyed the preparation and the hard work and the dedication that I had to make to try to be one of the best receivers to have ever played the game."

STATISTICS

JERRY RICE
POSITION: Wide receiver

FULL NAME: Jerry Lee Rice
BORN: October 13, 1962, Starkville, Mississippi
HEIGHT: 6'2"
HEIGHT: 200 lbs.
COLLEGE: Mississippi Valley State University

TEAMS: San Francisco Giants (1985–2000), Oakland Raiders (2001–2004), Seattle Seahawks (2004)

YEAR	TEAM	G	REC	YARDS	Y/R	TD
1985	SF	16	49	927	18.9	3
1986	SF	16	86	1,570	18.3	15
1987	SF	12	65	1,078	16.6	22
1988	SF	16	64	1,306	20.4	9
1989	SF	16	82	1,483	18.1	17
1990	SF	16	100	1,502	15.0	13
1991	SF	16	80	1,206	15.1	14
1992	SF	16	84	1,201	14.3	10
1993	SF	16	98	1,503	15.3	15
1994	SF	16	112	1,499	13.4	13
1995	SF	16	122	1,848	15.1	15
1996	SF	16	108	1,254	11.6	8
1997	SF	2	7	78	11.1	1
1998	SF	16	82	1,157	14.1	9
1999	SF	16	67	830	12.4	5

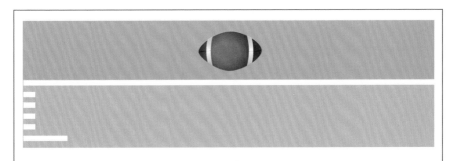

YEAR	TEAM	G	REC	YARDS	Y/R	TD
2000	SF	16	75	805	10.7	7
2001	OAK	16	83	1,139	13.7	9
2002	OAK	16	92	1,211	13.2	7
2003	OAK	16	63	869	13.8	2
2004	OAK	6	5	67	13.4	0
2004	SEA	11	25	362	14.5	3
CAREER		303	1,549	22,895	14.8	197

CHRONOLOGY

1962	October 13 Is born in Starkville, Mississippi.
1978–1980	Plays football at B.L. Moor High School; is an All-State selection at wide receiver in his senior year.
1981–1985	Attends Mississippi Valley State University.
1983 season	Sets NCAA marks for receptions (102) and receiving yards (1,450).
1984 season	Sets NCAA record for touchdowns (27) and breaks own records for receptions (112) and receiving yards (1,845); finishes ninth in Heisman Trophy voting.
1985	Drafted with the No. 16 pick by the San Francisco 49ers; is the third wide receiver taken.

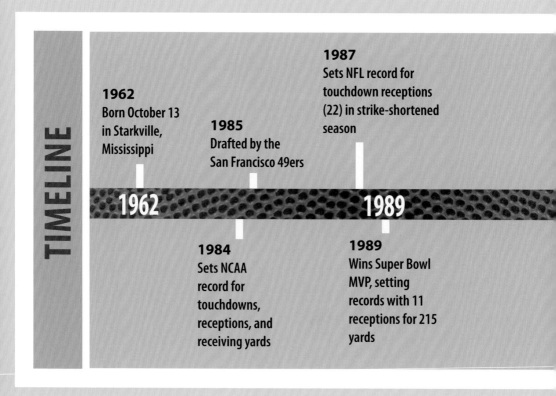

TIMELINE

1962
Born October 13 in Starkville, Mississippi

1985
Drafted by the San Francisco 49ers

1987
Sets NFL record for touchdown receptions (22) in strike-shortened season

1962

1989

1984
Sets NCAA record for touchdowns, receptions, and receiving yards

1989
Wins Super Bowl MVP, setting records with 11 receptions for 215 yards

1985 season   Wins NFC Rookie of the Year award.

1986 season   Leads the NFL in receiving yards (1,570) and touchdowns (15); begins streak of 11 straight Pro Bowls

1987   June 7 Daughter Jaqui Bonet is born.
September 8 Marries Jackie Mitchell.

1987 season   Sets NFL record for touchdown receptions (22) in strike-shortened season; sets records for touchdown catches in consecutive games (13); wins NFL Player of the Year award.

1988–1989 season   Averages career-high 20.4 yards per catch; San Francisco defeats Cincinnati Bengals in Super Bowl

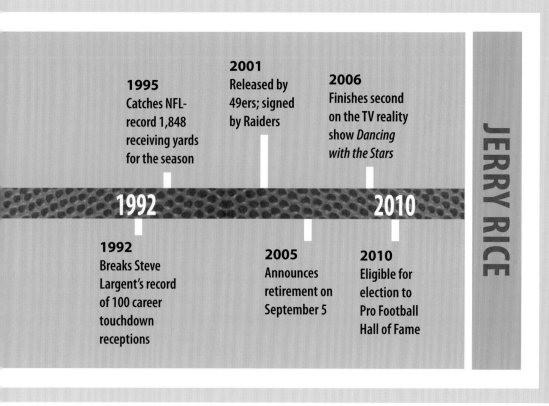

1995
Catches NFL-record 1,848 receiving yards for the season

2001
Released by 49ers; signed by Raiders

2006
Finishes second on the TV reality show *Dancing with the Stars*

1992

2010

1992
Breaks Steve Largent's record of 100 career touchdown receptions

2005
Announces retirement on September 5

2010
Eligible for election to Pro Football Hall of Fame

JERRY RICE

XXIII, 20-16; Rice wins Super Bowl MVP, setting records with 11 passes for 215 yards.

Coach Bill Walsh retires; is replaced by George Seifert.

1989–1990 season San Francisco defeats Denver Broncos in Super Bowl XXIV, 55-10; Rice catches seven passes for 148 yards and three touchdowns.

1990 season Catches 13 passes for 225 yards and five touchdowns against Atlanta Falcons; leads NFL in receptions (100), receiving yards (1,502), and touchdown receptions (13).

1991 July 27 Son Jerry, Jr., is born.

1992 season Breaks Steve Largent's record of 100 career touchdown receptions.

1993 season Catches 98 passes for 1,503 yards and 15 touchdowns; named NFL Offensive Player of the Year for the second time.

1994–1995 season Breaks Jim Brown's record for career touchdowns in first game of season; for season, catches 112 passes for 1,499 yards and 13 touchdowns; San Francisco defeats San Diego Chargers in Super Bowl XXIX, 49-26; catches 10 passes for 149 yards and three touchdowns in the Super Bowl.

1995 season Catches career-high 122 passes for an NFL-record 1,848 receiving yards; finishes second to Brett Favre in NFL MVP voting; breaks Art Monk's career record for most pass receptions (942); breaks James Lofton's record for most receiving yards (14,004).

1996 May 16 Daughter Jada Symone is born.

1996 season Catches pass No. 1,000 of his career.

1997 season	Tears ligaments in left knee; misses 14 games because of injury for first time in career.
1998 season	Comes back from injury to make Pro Bowl for twelfth time; oldest player to record more than 1,000 receiving yards.
2001	June Released by San Francisco 49ers; signed by Oakland Raiders.
2001 season	Catches 83 passes for 1,139 yards and nine touchdowns for the Raiders.
2002–2003 season	Makes Pro Bowl for the thirteenth (and last) time with 92 receptions for 1,211 yards and seven touchdowns; Tampa Bay Buccaneers defeat Oakland Raiders in Super Bowl XXVII, 48-21; catches five passes for 77 yards and one touchdown (first player ever to catch a touchdown pass in four Super Bowls).
2004 season	Traded from Raiders to Seattle Seahawks for a seventh-round draft pick.
2005	September 5 Retires after preseason training camp with Denver Broncos; holds more than 30 NFL records at time of retirement.
2006	Achieves new popularity by finishing second on the TV reality show *Dancing with the Stars*.
	Inducted into the College Football Hall of Fame.
2007	December Announces separation from wife after 20 years of marriage.
2010	Eligible for election to the Pro Football Hall of Fame.

GLOSSARY

audible   When the quarterback changes a play at the line of scrimmage by calling out a predetermined set of signals.

cornerback   A defensive back who lines up near the line of scrimmage across from a wide receiver. The cornerback's primary job is to disrupt passing routes, to defend against short and medium passes, and to contain the rusher on rushing plays.

defensive back   A cornerback or safety position on the defensive team; commonly defends against wide receivers on passing plays. Generally there are four defensive backs playing at a time.

draft   The selection of collegiate players for entrance into the National Football League. Typically, the team with the worst record in the previous season picks first in the draft.

end zone   The area between the end line and the goal line, bounded by the sidelines.

field goal   A scoring play of three points made by kicking the ball through the goalposts in the opponent's end zone.

fumble   When any offensive player loses possession of the ball before the play is blown dead.

free agent   A professional player who is not under contract with any football team. He may sign with any team he chooses.

flanker   A receiver who usually lines up outside the tight end, off the line of scrimmage.

handoff   The act of giving the ball to another player; generally occurs when the quarterback hands the ball to a running back, but it can take place between any two teammates.

Heisman Trophy   An award presented annually to the most outstanding player in Division I-A college football.

holding   A penalty in which one player keeps another from advancing by grabbing him and holding him back.

Offensive holding is a 10-yard penalty, and the down is repeated. Defensive holding results in a five-yard penalty and an automatic first down.

interception   A pass that is caught by a defensive player, giving his team the ball.

ligament   A sheet or band of tough, fibrous tissue that connects bones or cartilage at a joint or that holds an organ of the body in place.

linebacker   A player position on defense. Linebackers typically play one to six yards behind the defensive linemen. Most defenses use either three or four linebackers.

line of scrimmage   The imaginary line that stretches across the field and separates the two teams before the snap; before a play, teams line up on either side of the line of scrimmage.

offensive line   The offensive players who line up on the line of scrimmage. Their primary job is to block the defensive players.

patella   The kneebone.

penalty   Punishment for an infraction of the rules.

personal foul   A flagrant illegal act that is deemed to risk the health of other players. Personal fouls include unnecessary roughness and blows to the head. Such a foul results in a 15-yard penalty.

Pro Bowl   The all-star game of the NFL, played a week after the Super Bowl. Players are voted to the Pro Bowl by coaches, fellow players, and fans. Each group's ballots count for one-third of the vote.

quarterback   The offensive player who receives the ball from the center at the start of each play. The quarterback will hand off the ball, pass the ball, or run it himself.

reception   When a player catches a pass.

reverse   A play in which a running back takes a handoff from the quarterback and then turns and runs in a lateral motion behind the line of scrimmage before handing off to a receiver who is running in the opposite direction.

rookie   A player in his first year as a professional.

running back   An offensive player who runs with the football; also known as a tailback, halfback, or fullback.

secondary   The defensive players who line up behind the linebackers and defend the pass.

shotgun offense   A passing formation in which the quarterback stands five yards behind the center before the snap; the shotgun allows a quarterback to scan the defense from behind the line of scrimmage.

slant   In a slant route, the receiver runs straight up the field a few yards, plants his outside foot, and turns 45 degrees toward the quarterback. The route is a staple of the West Coast offense.

split end   A receiver who lines up on the line of scrimmage several yards outside the offensive linemen.

tendonitis   Inflammation of the tendon. The tendon is a tough cord or band of connective tissue that unites a muscle to another part, such as a bone.

tight end   An offensive player who lines up on the line of scrimmage next to the offensive tackle. Tight ends are used as blockers during running plays and either run a route or stay in to block during passing plays.

touchdown   A play worth six points in which any part of the ball while legally in the possession of a player crosses the plane of the opponent's goal line. A touchdown allows the team a chance for one extra point by kicking the ball or for two points by running or passing the ball into the end zone.

turnover   A loss of possession of the ball by either a fumble or an interception.

West Coast offense   An offensive philosophy that uses short, high-percentage passes as the core of a ball-control offense.

wide receiver   A player position on offense. He is split wide (usually about 10 yards) from the formation and plays on the line of scrimmage as a split end or one yard off as a flanker.

yard   One yard of linear distance in the direction of one of the two goals. A field is 100 yards. Typically, a team is required to advance at least 10 yards in order to get a new set of downs.

BIBLIOGRAPHY

BOOKS

Brenner, Richard. *The Complete Super Bowl Story: Games I–XXIV*. Syosset, N.Y.: East End Publishing, 1990.

Evans, Edward. *Jerry Rice: Touchdown Talent*. Minneapolis: Lerner, 1993.

Naden, Corinne, and Rose Blue. *Jerry Rice*. New York: Chelsea House Publishers, 1994.

Owens, Thomas. *Jerry Rice: Speedy Wide Receiver*. New York: Power Kids, 1997.

Rambeck, Richard. *Jerry Rice*. Plymouth, Minn.: Child's World, 1996.

Rice, Jerry, and Brian Curtis. *Go Long! My Journey Beyond the Game and the Fame*. New York: Ballantine, 2007.

Rice, Jerry, and Michael Silver. *Rice*. New York: St. Martin's Griffin, 1996.

Thornley, Stew. *Jerry Rice: Star Wide Receiver*. Springfield, N.J.: Enslow Publishers, 1998.

ARTICLES

Barra, Allen. "Joe Montana, Tarnished Hero." Salon.com, August 4, 2000. Available online at *http://dir.salon.com/news/sports/col/barra/2000/08/04/replacements/index.html*.

Battista, Judy. "Rice, at 42, Concedes His Time Has Passed." *The New York Times*, September 6, 2005. Available online at *http://www.nytimes.com/2005/09/06/sports/football/06rice.html*.

Blackistone, Kevin. "Coaches Totten and Cooley at It Again." *Dallas Morning News*, October 14, 2005. Available online at *http://www.dallasnews.com/sharedcontent/dws/spt/columnists/kblackistone/stories/101505dnspoblackistonecol.21afdc92.html*.

Carter, Bob. "49ers Era Was Rice Era." ESPN Classic. Available online at *http://espn.go.com/classic/biography/s/Rice_Jerry.html*.

Dietz, David and Howard Arceneaux. "DeBartolo Guilty of Felony." *San Francisco Chronicle*, October 7, 1998. Available online at *http://www.sfgate.com/cgi-bin/article.cgi?file=/chronicle/archive/1998/10/07/MN4647.DTL*.

"Edward John DeBartolo, Jr.—The 400 Richest Americans." *Forbes*, 2005. Available online at *http://www.forbes.com/lists/2005/54/U1LO.html*.

FitzGerald, Tom. "Former 49er Head Coach Bill Walsh Dies." *San Francisco Chronicle*, July 30, 2007. Available online at *http://www.sfgate.com/cgi-bin/article.cgi?f=/c/a/2007/07/30/BAG57LR8OK21.DTL*.

"Football's 100 Greatest Players." *The Sporting News*, 1999. Available online at *http://archive.sportingnews.com/nfl/100/*.

"From Jerry Rice to Randy Moss and Beyond: Perceiving Yesterday's Athlete and Today's." January 3, 2008. Available online at *http://sports.aol.com/fanhouse/2008/01/03/jerry-rice-calls-randy-moss-comments-a-slap-in-the-face-but-th/*

Gay, Nancy. "Tim Brown Retires." *San Francisco Chronicle*, July 19, 2005. Available online at *http://www.sfgate.com/cgi-bin/article.cgi?f=/c/a/2005/07/19/SPG0CDQ4G31.DTL*.

George, Thomas. "Just No Catching Up with 49ers' Rice." *The New York Times*, December 3, 1990. Available online at *http://query.nytimes.com/gst/fullpage.html?res=9C0CE2DE163AF930A35751C1A966958260*.

Gosselin, Rick. "Route-Runners Are on NFL's Cutting Edge." *Dallas Morning News*, November 16, 2006. Available online at *http://www.chiefshuddle.com/forums/lofiversion/index.php/t28764.html*.

"Governor Ross Barnett's Proclamation to the People of Mississippi." American RadioWorks, September 13, 1962. Available online at *http://americanradioworks.publicradio.org/features/prestapes/barnettspeech.html*.

Gramm, Cynthia, and John Schnell. "Difficult Choices: Crossing the Picket Line During the 1987 National Football League Strike." *Journal of Labor Economics* Vol. 12, No. 1 (January 1994), 41–73.

Hack, Damon. "Rice Eager to Show Seahawks He's Still Young Enough." *The New York Times*, October 20, 2004. Available online at *http://www.nytimes.com/2004/10/20/sports/football/20rice.html*.

"Jerry Rice Calls Randy Moss Comments a Slap in the Face." AOL Fanhouse, January 3, 2008. Available online at *http://sports.aol.com/fanhouse/2008/01/03/jerry-rice-calls-randy-moss-comments-a-slap-in-the-face-but-th/*.

"Jerry Rice—Superstar in the Making." Available online at *http://sports.jrank.org/pages/3844/Rice-Jerry-Superstar-in-Making.html*.

Kroichick, Ron. "Glory Has Its Price." *San Francisco Chronicle.* January 21, 2007. Available online at *http://www.sfgate.com/cgi-bin/article.cgi?f=/c/a/2007/01/21/SPG6JNM6MN1.DTL*.

"Members: Nationally Prominent Athletes Giving Back." Athletes for a Better World. Available online at *http://www.aforbw.com/members/npathletesgivingback.asp*.

"Mississippi Mud." *Time*, September 7, 1959. Available online at *http://www.time.com/time/magazine/article/0,9171,825882,00.html*.

"No. 2: Rice Ran Away from the Field with Grace." *USA Today*, July 7, 2007. Available online at *http://www.usatoday.com/sports/football/nfl/2007-07-20-no-2-jerry-rice_N.htm*.

Ostler, Scott. "Top of the Line: Weird Ways and Times of a Football Team." *San Francisco Chronicle*, July 31, 2007. Available online at *http://www.sfgate.com/cgi-bin/article.cgi?f=/c/a/2007/07/31/SP6TRA0KT3.DTL.*

Owens, Jason. "Glory Days for Willie Totten." CSTV.com, September 22, 2005. Available online at *http://www.cstv.com/sports/m-footbl/stories/092205abm.html.*

Pasquarelli, Len. "An Offense By Any Other Name . . ." ESPN.com, October 25, 2007. Available online at *http://espn.go.com/nfl/s/westcoast/history.html.*

"Rice Reception Streak Snapped at 274 Games." *Cincinnati Enquirer*, September 20, 2004. Available online at *http://bengals.enquirer.com/2004/09/20/ben2nte.html.*

"Rodgers Performs for Gruden." *Oakland Tribune*, April 10, 2005. Available online at *http://findarticles.com/p/articles/mi_qn4176/is_20050410/ai_n15820392.*

"Seahawks Lose to Rams for Third Time This Season," ESPN.com, January 8, 2005. Available online at *http://sports.espn.go.com/nfl/recap?gameId=250108026.*

Soliday, Bill. "'87 NFL Strike Paved Way for Free Agency." *Contra Costa Times*, November 27, 2007.

Tanier, Mike. "Too Deep Zone: Jerry Rice, Rookie Bust." November 17, 2006. Available online at *http://www.footballoutsiders.com/2006/11/17/ramblings/too-deep-zone/4554/.*

Telander, Rick. "Superb!" *Sports Illustrated*, February 6, 1995. Available online at *http://sportsillustrated.cnn.com/football/features/superbowl/archives/29/.*

Timanus, Eddie. "1-AA Feats Give Rice Call to College Football Hall of Fame." *USA Today*, August 9, 2006. Available online at *http://www.usatoday.com/sports/college/football/2006-08-09-rice-hall-of-fame_x.htm.*

Ulman, Howard. "Jerry Rice Praises Randy Moss in Pursuit of Record." *USA Today*, December 13, 2007. Available online at *http://www.usatoday.com/sports/football/2007-12-13-2560455191_x.htm*.

Wagaman, Michael. "Sharing the Spotlight." *Pro Football Weekly*, July 30, 2001. Available online at *http://archive.profootballweekly.com/content/archives2001/features_2001/wagaman_073001.asp*.

FURTHER READING

BOOKS

Barber, Phil, and Michael Zagaris. *We Were Champions: The 49ers' Dynasty in Their Own Words*. Chicago: Triumph Books, 2002.

Craig, Roger, with Matt Maiocco. *Tales from the San Francisco 49ers Sideline*. Champaign, Ill.: Sports Publishing, 2004.

Harris, David. *The Genius: How Bill Walsh Reinvented Football and Created an NFL Dynasty*. New York: Random House, 2008.

McDonell, Chris. *The Football Game I'll Never Forget: 100 NFL Stars' Stories*. Richmond Hill, Ontario: Firefly Books, 2004.

McDonough, Will, ed. *The NFL Century: The Complete Story of the National Football League, 1920–2000*. New York: Smithmark, 1999.

Moyer, Susan, ed. *Bill Walsh: Remembering "The Genius": 1931–2007*. Champaign, Ill.: Sports Publishing, 2007.

Palmer, Pete, et. al. *The ESPN Pro Football Encyclopedia*. 2nd ed. New York: Sterling, 2007.

Walsh, Bill, et. al., *Bill Walsh: Finding the Winning Edge*. Champaign, Ill.: Sagamore Publishing, 1997.

Yost, Mark. *Tailgating, Sacks, and Salary Caps: How the NFL Became the Most Successful Sports League in History*. Chicago: Kaplan, 2006.

WEB SITES

Official Site of the National Football League
http://www.nfl.com

Official Site of the San Francisco 49ers
http://www.sf49ers.com

Official Web Site of Jerry Rice
http://www.jerryricefootball.com

Pro Football Hall of Fame
http://www.profootballhof.com

Pro Football Reference
http://www.pro-football-reference.com

PICTURE CREDITS

INDEX

ABOUT THE AUTHOR

JON STERNGASS is the author of *First Resorts: Pursuing Pleasure at Saratoga Springs, Newport, and Coney Island* (Johns Hopkins University Press, 2001). He currently is a freelance writer specializing in children's nonfiction books; his most recent works are a biography of Dan Marino and a history of Filipino Americans. Born and raised in Brooklyn, Jon Sterngass has a B.A. in history from Franklin and Marshall College, an M.A. in medieval history from the University of Wisconsin-Milwaukee, and a Ph.D in American history from City University of New York. He has lived in Saratoga Springs, New York, for 16 years with his wife, Karen Weltman, and sons Eli (14) and Aaron (11). One of his fondest memories as a football fan is watching the Blue-Gray Game with his brother Bobby in the old house on East 24th Street and Avenue J.